ESSAYS OF A CATHOLIC

BOOKS BY HILAIRE BELLOC

Available From The Publisher
In This Series

Europe and the Faith

William The Conqueror

The Crusades

How the Reformation Happened

Characters of the Reformation

Essays of a Catholic

The Great Heresies

Survivals and New Arrivals

The Crisis of Civilization

ESSAYS OF A CATHOLIC

By

Hilaire Belloc

"Truth comes by conflict."

TAN BOOKS AND PUBLISHERS, INC.
Rockford, Illinois 61105

First published in 1931 by The Macmillan Company, New York.

ISBN: 0-89555-463-1

Library of Congress Catalog Card No.: 92-60964

Printed and bound in the United States of America.

TAN BOOKS AND PUBLISHERS, INC.
P.O. Box 424
Rockford, Illinois 61105

1992

To

CHARLOTTE BALFOUR

TABLE OF CONTENTS

PREFACE

The papers collected in the following pages are from many sources; they are, as the reader will discover, of very different lengths; they touch upon subjects of very different kinds and very different degrees of importance. I must express my particular gratitude to the proprietors and editor of the *Universe* for their permission to incorporate parts of certain essays which appeared in their columns, forming about one third of the book. The *Universe* has given hospitality to my work for many years and also given it the advantage of appearing before the very large and increasing public which it reaches: we all owe it gratitude for the great work it is doing. To the Essays which thus appeared in the *Universe* I have added, in most cases rewritten much as well as expanded. One of the essays appeared on the other side of the Atlantic in connection with a controversy between the Church and the wealthy Puritans of the northeastern States in an organ peculiarly their own. This also ("The Church and the Modern State") I have had to rewrite somewhat; I have included it because the subject is of general interest wherever the Church and State are today in conflict. The "Letter to Dean Inge," which I have also retouched slightly, but not in more than a dozen lines, first appeared—strangely enough!—in the *Evening Standard* of London, though it was then under the same proprietorship as it is today. Two of the papers, which break, I believe, fresh ground and which I confess I took special pains over, are that on "Usury," and the one called "Science as the Enemy of Truth."

I must apologize for the personal tone in each of the papers here printed: I can write in no other way, and, indeed, I prefer in reading the writings of others to discover a similar note myself. It has the advantage in the present case of disengaging anyone else of my communion from views I may express, and I hope the reader will recognize my intention in the choice of the title. I have not put forward this book as the Essays of a Catholic in general, which would be presumptuous, but only as the Essays of one chance Catholic, who is but a layman, and, what is more, a layman living in England, where Catholic things appear and live with difficulty.

I do not know whether I ought to apologize for the fact that all these papers deal only with what may be called the externals of religion, are even in great part political, and without exception controversial. I have perhaps no faculty for dealing on paper with the more essential, the all-important, interior things of Catholic life. If ever I have dealt or shall deal with them I am sure I should not sign my name.

H. BELLOC

Kings Land
Shipley, Horsham
20th May, 1931

The New Paganism

Our civilization developed as a Catholic civilization. It developed and matured as a Catholic thing. With the loss of the Faith it will slip back not only into Paganism, but into barbarism with the accompaniments of Paganism, and especially the institution of slavery. It will find gods to worship, but they will be evil gods as were those of the older savage Paganism before it began its advance towards Catholicism. The road downhill is the same as the road up the hill. It is the same road; but to go down back into the marshes again is a very different thing from coming up from the marshes into pure air. All things return to their origin. A living organic being, whether a human body or a whole state of society, turns at last into its original elements if life be not maintained in it. But in that process of return there is a phase of corruption which is very unpleasant. That phase the modern world outside the Catholic Church has arrived at.

1
THE NEW PAGANISM

We call Paganism an absence of the Christian revelation. That is why we distinguish between Paganism and the different heresies; that is why we give the name of Christian to imperfect and distorted Christians, who only possess a part of Catholic truth and usually add to it doctrines which are contradictory of Catholic truth. Moreover, the word "Christian," though so vague as to be dangerous, has this much reality about it, that there is something different between the general atmosphere or savor of any society or person or literature which can be called Christian at all and those which are wholly lacking in any part of Christian doctrine. For a Christian man or society is one that has some part of Catholicism left in him. But when every shred of Catholicism is lost we call that state of things "Unchristian."

Now, it must be evident to everybody by this time that, with the attack on Faith and the Church at the Reformation, the successful rebellion of so many and their secession from United Christendom, there began a process which could only end in the complete loss of all Catholic doctrine and morals by the deserters. That consummation we are today reaching. It took a long time to come about, but come about it has. We have but to look around us to see that there are, spreading over what used to be the Christian world, larger and larger areas over which the Christian spirit has wholly failed; is absent. I mean by "larger areas" both larger moral and larger physical areas, but especially larger moral areas. There are now whole groups of books, whole bodies of men, which are definitely Pagan, and these are beginning to join up into larger groups. It is like the freezing over of a pond, which begins in patches of ice; the patches unite to form wide sheets, till at last the whole is one solid surface. There are considerable masses of literature in the modern world, of philosophy and history (and especially of fiction), which are Pagan and they are coalescing—to form a *corpus* of anti-Christian influence. It is not so much that they deny the Incarnation and the Resurrection, not even that they ignore doctrine. It is rather that they contradict and oppose the old inherited Christian system of morals to which people used to adhere long after they had given up definite doctrine.

This New Paganism is already a world of its own. It bulks large, and it is certainly going to spread and occupy more and more of modern life. It is exceedingly important that we should judge rightly and in good time of what its effects will probably be, for we are going to come under the influence of those effects to some extent, and our children will come very strongly under their influence. Those effects are already impressing themselves profoundly upon the Press, conversation, laws, building, and intimate habits of our time.

There are two ways in which this is happening; according to whether the New Paganism is at work in a Catholic or a non-Catholic country. It is happening in Catholic countries by the separation of a Pagan set from the rest of the citizens. In those countries the full body of Christian doctrine, that is, Catholicism, puts up a permanent and successful resistance. Its consequences in morals are accepted by masses of people who do not practice the Catholic religion or who are indifferent to its doctrines, and this resistance shows no sign of weakening; not everywhere are the governments of Catholic countries in sympathy with Catholic tradition, however vague, but in these countries the laws defending morals and the general habits of people outside the Pagan set may properly be called anti-Pagan.

But though the way in which the New Paganism is establishing itself differs according to whether the society in which it takes root was originally Catholic or Protestant, it is everywhere of much the same tone, and its effects are very similar, whether you find them in Italy or in Berlin, in an English novel or a

French one; and the marks peculiar to Paganism are very clearly apparent in all.

Of these marks the two most prominent are, first, the postulate that man is sufficient to himself—that is, the omission of the idea of Grace; the second (a consequence of this), despair.

The New Paganism is the resultant of two forces which have converged to produce it: appetite and the sense of doom. Of the forces which impelled it into being, the appeal of the senses to be released from restriction through the denial of the Faith is so obvious that none will contest it, the only controversy being upon whether this removal of restriction upon sensual enjoyment, declining every form of reticence and exercising the fullest license for what is called "self-expression," is of good or of evil effect upon the individual and upon society. The Christian scheme is still close enough even to the most Pagan of the New Pagans to be familiar, and the social atmosphere which it created still endures as a memory, or as a rejected experience, in their lives. That social atmosphere insisted on a number of restrictions. Of course, no society could exist in which there were not a great number of restrictions, but the restrictions imposed by Christian morals were severe and numerous, and most of them are meaningless to those who have abandoned Christian doctrine, because morals are the fruit of doctrine.

It is not only in sexual matters (the first that will be cited in this connection), but in canons of taste, in social conduct, traditional canons of beauty in verse, prose, or the plastic arts that there is outbreak. The restriction and, therefore, the effort necessary for lucidity in prose, for scansion in poetry and, according to our tradition, for rhyme in most poetry—the restrictions imposed by reverence for age, for certain relationships such as those between parent and child, for the respect of property as a right—and all the rest of it are broken through. A license in act and a necessarily more extended license in speech are therefore the mark of the New Paganism.

But to this negative force must be added a positive one to explain what is happening, and that positive one is a philosophy which may be called Monist, or Fatalist, or Determinist, or by one of any number of names all signifying either the absence of conscious Will from the universe or the presence of only one such Will therein.

The true origin of this attitude of mind in modern times is the powerful genius of Calvin, though those who most suffer his influence would most strenuously deny their subjection to it, partly because they have never read him, much more because they do not see it in their daily papers, and most of all because Calvin is vaguely mixed up in their minds with an interest in theology, which science is thought to have exploded—there is also perhaps some little distaste for Calvin because he was a Frenchman, but as that deplorable fact is never emphasized it cannot count for much. Calvin, then, is at the fountainhead of this new sense of Doom. But behind Calvin the fatalist attitude is an attitude as old, of course, as the hills. It is a temptation to which the human intellect has yielded on important occasions from as far back as we can trace its recorded experience and definitions. To the mind in that mood all things are part of an unchangeable process following from cause to effect immutably.

What else may have produced this positive force of fatalism, itself a main factor in the new Paganism, I will not here discuss; I have said more about it in my essay on "Science as the Enemy of Truth." I am here only concerned with observing its presence; but I will say this much: that one very powerful agent in producing this mood is the desire to be rid of responsibility.

A direct consequence of this philosophy, though again it is a consequence furiously denied by its victims, is the elimination of right and wrong. Our actions do not depend upon our own wills; those who think that they proceed from an act of the will suffer an illusion; human action, from what used to be called the noblest self-sacrifice to the basest commercial swindling, is the inevitable result of forces over which the perpetrator has no control—or, as Dean Swift has admirably put it in that great masterpiece, *The Tale of a Tub,* "It was ordained some three days before the Creation that my nose should come against this lamp post."

It is true that the professors of this creed are illogical; for no one gives louder vent to moral indignation than themselves, especially when they are denouncing the cruelties or ineptitudes of believers in moral responsibility, but then, as the denial of the human reason is also part of their creed, or, at any rate, the denial of its value as the instrument for the discovery of truth, they will not be seriously disturbed by the incongruity of their outbursts; for what is incongruous or illogical is not to them blameworthy or ridiculous—rather in their mouths does the world "logical" connote something absurd and empty.

Now, it is with this element of Monism that there enters a highly practical consideration in our survey of the New Paganism. It is this: the New Paganism is in process of building up a society of its own, wherein will be apparent two features novel in what used to be Christendom. Those two features have already appeared and will spread each in its own sphere, the one in the sphere of law—that is, of coercive enactment—the other in the sphere of *status,* that is, in the organization of society.

In the first sphere, that of positive law, the New Paganism has already begun to produce and cannot but produce more and more a mass of restrictive legislation. It is a paradox, of course, that such restrictive legislation should be bred from a mood which proceeded originally from rebellion against restriction, but the fact is undoubted—it is before all our eyes. With the denial of the will there necessarily appears the questioning of any content to the word "freedom." In a Christian society you were free to do a number of acts, for some of which you could be punished under Christian laws, for others of which no state or other authority could punish you, but which were opposed to the social atmosphere in which you lived. But the New Paganism will tend, not to punish, but to restrain with fetters; to prevent action, to impose coercive bonds. It will be at issue more and more with human dignity. It has already, in certain provinces (the Calvinist canton of Vaud in Switzerland is an example), enacted what is called "the sterilization of the unfit" as a positive law. It has not yet enacted, though it has already proposed and will certainly in time enact, legislation for the restriction of births. Not only in these, but in many other departments of life, one after another, will this mechanical network spread and bind those subject to it under a compulsion which cannot be escaped.

In the sphere of social texture the New Paganism must also inevitably and of its nature, wherever it gives its tone to society, reintroduce that status of slavery from which our civilization sprang and which only very gradually disappeared under the influence of the Christian ethic.

This revival of slavery must not be confused with the spread of mechanical restriction applicable to all. They are cousins, but they are not identical. Slavery is the compulsion of one man or set of men to work for the benefit of others. It is a compulsion to work, backed by the arms of the State. The way has been prepared for it by that already half-Pagan thing—industrial capitalism, of which I write on a later page; and the steps whereby the New Paganism will achieve slavery develop naturally from industrial capitalism. It is a thesis I have developed at greater length in my book, *The Servile State;* I here only touch on it as a main social result to which the New Paganism will give birth. That this novel status will bear the name "slavery" I doubt; for it is in the nature of mankind, when they are proceeding to call that good which once they called evil, to avoid the old evil name. In the same way fornication is not called fornication but "companionate marriage." Probably slavery, when it comes, will be called "permanent employment"; and a century hence, a rich man will say to his friends, talking of his new gardener: "He's a permanent. Paid for him at the Bureau only last Thursday."

In the form of security and sufficiency for the men who labor to the profit of others, and in the form of registering and controlling them in the form of an organized public supervision of their labor, slavery is already afoot. When slavery shall succeed it will succeed through the acquiescence of those who will be enslaved, for they will prefer sufficiency and security with enslavement, to freedom, responsibility, insecurity and the threat of insufficiency.

As yet, during the transition, there is an illogical, and therefore an ephemeral mixture of the old and the new. The old freedom sufficiently survives in the mind of the wage earner to give him the illusion that, while accepting insurance and maintenance from the capitalist state, he can still be a full citizen. He thinks he can have his cake and eat it too. He is mistaken. The great capitalists who procured these regulations from the politicians knew what they were at. They were catching their proletariat in a net, and now they hold it fast.

The New Paganism will then, I say, give us, in those societies over which it shall obtain the control of the mind, increasing restriction against general freedom and increasing restriction against the particular freedom which left some equality between the man who worked and the man who exploited him under a contract—it will replace that idea of contract by the older idea of status. In saying this, my object is to point out that the discussion of the New Paganism is not a mere academic discussion, but, as I have called it, one of immediate practical importance. If we adopt it we must be prepared for its consequences; if we abhor those consequences, it is our business to fight the New Paganism vigorously.

And here I have, as on so many other points, a quarrel with those moderns who will make of religion an individual thing (and no Catholic can evade the corporate quality of religion), telling us that its object being personal holiness and the salvation of the individual soul, it can have no concern with politics. On the contrary, the concern of religion with politics is inevitable. Not that the Christian doctrine and ethic rejects any one of the three classical forms of government—democracy, aristocracy or monarchy, or any mixture of them—but that it does reject certain features in society which are opposed to the Christian social products, and are opposed to them because they spring from a denial of free will.

The battle for right doctrine in theology is always also a battle for the preservation of definite social things (institutions, habits) following from right doctrine; nor is there anything more contemptible intellectually than the attitude of those who imagine that because doctrine must be stated in abstract terms it therefore has no practical application nor any real fruit in the real world of real men. Contrariwise, difference in doctrine is at the root of all political and social differences; therefore is the struggle for or against true doctrine the most vital of struggles.

But apart from these aspects of the New Paganism there is another which I confess I happen to feel myself closely concerned with. It is the connection between the New Paganism and that lure of the antique world, which is of such power over all generous minds, and especially upon those who are in love with beauty.

It is in my judgment an argument which has certainly been of powerful effect in the immediate past, and will continue for some time longer, even in our declining culture, to be of powerful effect, that Paganism is to be sought, respected and achieved because our race, before the advent of the Catholic Church, wrote what it did, built what it did, chiselled what it did, and everywhere created the loveliness to which we Christians are the heirs. Yet this attraction of the antique world I conceive to be a dangerous decoy, leading us on to things very different from and very much worse than that classic Paganism from which we all descend.

I know that to affirm the connection between the New Paganism and a wistfulness for the Old will sound in most modern ears fantastic, because most modern people who fall into the New Paganism know nothing about the Paganism of antiquity; there never was a time when educated men had a larger proportion among them ignorant of Latin and Greek, since first Greek was taught in the universities of Western Europe; and there was certainly never a time during the last two thousand years when the mass of people, the workers, were given less knowledge of the past and were less in sympathy with tradition.

Nonetheless, it is true that the idea of Pagan antiquity as a model runs through the whole new movement. With a few scholars it is at first-hand, with most people at second, third, fourth or fifth; but it is there with everyone. There is a general knowledge that men were once free from the burden of Christian duty, and a widespread belief that when men were free from it, life was better because it was more rational and directed to things which they could all be sure of and test for themselves, such as the health of the body and physical comforts and pleasant surroundings, and the rest. To direct life again to these objects, making man once more sufficient to himself and treating temporal good as the supreme good, is the note of the New Paganism.

Now what seems to me by far the most important thing to point out in this connection is that the underlying assumption in all this is false. The New Paganism differs, and must differ radically, from the Old; its consequences in human life will be quite different; presumably much worse, and increasingly worse.

The reason of this is that you cannot undo an experience. You cannot cut off a man or a society from their past, and the world of Christendom has had the experience of the Faith. When it moves away from the Faith to return to Paganism again it is not doing the same thing, not producing the same emotions, not passing through the same process, not suffering the same reactions, as the old Paganism did, which was moving towards the Faith. It is one thing to go south from the Arctic towards the civilized parts of Europe; it is quite another thing to go north from the civilized parts of Europe to the Arctic. You are not merely returning to a place from which you started, you are going through a contrary series of emotions the whole time.

The New Paganism, should it ever become universal, or over whatever districts or societies it may become general, will never be what the Old Paganism was. It will be other, because it will be a corruption.

The Old Paganism was profoundly traditional; indeed, it had no roots except in tradition. Deep reverence for its own past and for the wisdom of its ancestry and pride therein were the very soul of the Old Paganism; that is why it formed so solid a foundation on which to build the Catholic Church, though that is also why it offered so long and determined a resistance to the growth of the Catholic Church. But the New Paganism has for its very essence contempt for tradition and contempt of ancestry. It respects perhaps nothing, but least of all does it respect the spirit of "Our fathers have told us."

The Old Paganism worshipped human things, but the noblest

human things, particularly reason and the sense of beauty. In these it rose to heights greater than have since been reached, perhaps, and certainly to heights as great as were ever reached by mere reason or in the mere production of beauty during the Christian centuries.

But the New Paganism despises reason, and boasts that it is attacking beauty. It presents with pride music that is discordant, building that is repellent, pictures that are a mere chaos, and it ridicules the logical process, so that, as I have said, it has made of the very word "logical" a sort of sneer.

The Old Paganism was of a sort that would be open, when due time came, to the authority of the Catholic Church. It had ears which at least would hear and eyes which at least would see; but the New Paganism not only has closed its senses, but is atrophying them, so that it aims at a state in which there shall be no ears to hear and no eyes to see.

The one was growing keener in its sight and its hearing; the other is declining towards a condition where the society it informs will be blind and deaf, even to the main natural pleasures of life and to temporal truths. It will be incapable of understanding what they are all about.

The Old Paganism had a strong sense of the supernatural. This sense was often turned to the wrong objects and always to insufficient objects, but it was keen and unfailing; all the poetry of the Old Paganism, even where it despairs, has this sense. And you may read in those of its writers who actively opposed religion, such as Lucretius, a fine religious sense of dignity and order. The New Paganism delights in superficiality, and conceives that it is rid of the evil as well as the good in what it believes to have been superstitions and illusions.

There it is quite wrong, and upon that note I will end. Men do not live long without gods; but when the gods of the New Paganism come they will not be merely insufficient, as were the gods of Greece, nor merely false; they will be evil. One might put it in a sentence, and say that the New Paganism, foolishly expecting satisfaction, will fall, before it knows where it is, into Satanism.

ON USURY

Usury does not mean high interest. It means any interest, however low, demanded for an unproductive loan. It is not only immoral (on which account it has been condemned by every moral code—Pagan—Mohammedan—or Catholic) but it is ultimately destructive of society. It has only been the rule of our commerce to take usury since the breakup of Europe following on the Reformation. Usury will destroy our society, but meanwhile there is no escape from it. We are coming near the end of its maleficent action, not through awaking to its evils but because it is reaching the end of its resources. The Great War loans, which are almost entirely usurious, have powerfully accelerated this process.

2

ON USURY

The modern world is organized on the principle that money of its nature breeds money. A sum of money lent has, according to our present scheme, a natural right to interest. That principle is false in economics as in morals. It ruined Rome, and it is bringing us to our end.

Supposing a man comes to you and says: "There is a field next to mine which is a very good building site; if I put up a good little house on it I shall be able to let that house at a net profit—all rates, taxes and repairs paid—of £100 a year. But I have no capital with which to build this house. The field will cost £50 and the house £950. Will you lend me £1,000, so that I can buy the field, put up the house, and enjoy this nice little income?" You would presumably answer, "Where do I come in? You get your £100 a year all right; but you only get it by my aid, and therefore I ought to share in the profits. Let us go fifty-fifty. You take £50 every year as your share for your knowledge of the opportunity and for your trouble, and hand me over the other £50. That will be five percent on my money, and I shall be content."

This answer, granted that property is a moral right, is a perfectly moral proposition. The borrower accepting that proposition certainly has no grievance. For a long time (theoretically, forever) you could go on drawing five percent on the money you lent, with a conscience at ease.

Now let us suppose that man comes to you and says: "I know the case of a man in middle age who has been suddenly stricken with a terrible ailment. Medical aid costing £1,000 will save his life, but he will never be able to do any more work. He has an annuity of £100 a year to keep him alive after the operation and subsequent treatment. Will you lend the £1,000? It will be paid back to you on his death, for his life has been insured in a lump payment for the amount of £1,000." You answer: "I will lend £1,000 to save his life, but I shall require of him half his annuity, that is £50 a year, for every year he may live henceforward; and he must scrape along as best he can on the remaining £50 of his annuity." That answer would make you feel a cad if you have any susceptibilities left, and if you have not—having already become a cad through the action of what the poet has called "the soul's long dues of hardening and decay"—it would be a caddish action all the same, though you might not be disturbed by it.

It seems therefore that there are conditions under which you may legitimately and morally lend £1,000 at five percent in perfect security of conscience, and others in which you cannot.

Now look at the matter from another angle.

When the American city of Boston was founded, three hundred years ago, a man in London proposing to emigrate thither left gold to the value of £1,000 with a London goldsmith, under a bond that the goldsmith might use the money until he or his heirs should demand it, but with the proviso that five percent on the capital should accrue at compound interest until it was withdrawn. The emigrant did not reappear. The goldsmith's business developed, as so many of them did, into a sort of bank as the seventeenth century wore on. By the beginning of the eighteenth it was a bank in due form, and its successor today is part of one of the great banking concerns of our time. The original deposit has gone on "fructifying," as the phrase goes, with the liability piling up, but no one claiming it.

At last, in this year 1931, an heir turns up and proves his title. The capital sum into which this modest investment of a thousand pounds at five percent has grown is to be paid over to him under an order of the court. Do you know how much it will come to?—More than twice the annual revenue of the United States today.

Let us take a less fantastic example, and perhaps it will be more convincing. Supposing a man to have lent £10,000 on mortgage at six percent upon an English gentleman's estate at the beginning of the American War of Independence, in 1776: the said estate to pay £600 a year to the lender. The debt is not pressed. The embarrassed gentleman is allowed to add to the principal the annual payments due, so that the whole sums up at the rate of six percent compound interest.

That is not at all an impossible supposition. Do you know what the mortgage-holder could demand of that estate today? Nearly five million pounds a year!

Neither of these examples could arise in practice because the law forbids such prolonged accumulation, but the very fact that the law has been compelled to do so, is proof that there is something wrong with the current notion everywhere acted upon, that money "earns" a certain rate of interest and has a moral right to it without regard to the way in which the capital is employed.

For what is common to all these illustrations is the patent fact that interest on a loan may, under some circumstances of time or extent, be a demand for an impossible tribute. It may under some circumstances be a tribute which is not morally due, because it does not represent an extra production of wealth due to the original investment. It is under some circumstances a demand for wealth which is not connected with the produce of the original investment, and the payment of which is therefore not a payment of part profit, but a payment to be made, if possible, out of whatever other wealth the debtor can obtain; and a tribute which, beyond a certain point, cannot even be paid at all, because the wherewithal to pay it is not present in society.

What are those circumstances? What are the conditions distinguishing a demand for payment of interest which is legitimate in morals from a demand which is illegitimate?

The distinction lies between a demand for part of the product of a productive loan, which is moral, and the immoral demand for either (1) interest on an unproductive loan, or (2) interest greater than the annual increment in real wealth which a productive loan creates. Such a demand "wears down"—"eats up"—

"drains dry" the wealth of the borrower, and that is why it is called Usury. A derivation inaccurate in philology, but sound in morals, rightly connects *"usura"* "usury," with the idea of destroying, "using up," rather than with the original idea of *"usus,"* "a use."

Usury, then, is a claiming of interest upon an unproductive loan, or of interest greater than the real increment produced by a productive loan. It is the claiming of something to which the lender has no right, as though I should say: "Pay me ten sacks of wheat a year for the rent of these fields" after the fields had been swallowed up by the sea, or after they had fallen to producing annually much less than ten sacks of wheat.

I must here reluctantly introduce a colloquial meaning of the word "Usury" which confuses thought. People talk of "usurious interest," meaning very high interest. It is obvious how the confusion arose. Very high interest is commonly greater than the real wealth produced even by a productive loan, and to demand it is, in effect, to demand more than the produce of the original loan; but there is nothing in the rate of interest *per se* which renders such interest usurious. You may demand one hundred percent on a loan and be well within your moral rights.

For instance, a small claim which was producing 500 ounces of gold a year has a sudden opportunity for producing 200 times as much, 100,000 ounces, if capital the equivalent of only 1,000 ounces can be obtained for development. The lender of that new capital is under no moral obligation to give all the vastly increased profits as a present to the borrower. He can legitimately claim his portion; he might well ask for half the new produce, that is 50,000 ounces per annum, 500 percent on his loan, for that very high interest would only come to half the new wealth produced. To ask for that 500 percent would not be an exaction of tribute from wealth that was not present, nor for wealth that was not created by the capital invested.

Strictly speaking, then, usury has nothing to do with the amount of interest demanded, but with the point whether there is or is not produced by the capital invested an increment at least equal to the tribute demanded.

If authority is asked for so obvious a position in morals it may be found in every great moral system sanctioned by the religious and permanent social philosophies adopted by men. Aristotle[1] forbids it, St. Thomas forbids it. The Mohammedan system of ethics condemns it (and in practice condemns it unintelligently because it forbids many loans that are useful[2]). In particular we have the luminous decision of the Fourth Lateran Council [1215].

So far, so good. Next let us note the very interesting development of modern times since the break-up of our common European moral and religious system at the Reformation. After that disaster usury gradually became admitted. It grew to be a general practice sanctioned by the laws, and the payment of it enforced by the civil magistrate. In England it was under the reign of Cecil, in the year 1571, that interest, though limited to ten percent, became legal without regard to the use made of the loan. The birth year of what may be called "Indiscriminate Usury" is 1609, when, under Calvinism, the Bank of Amsterdam started on its great career of stimulating fortunate capacity and ruining the unfortunate. In general the governments which broke away from the unity of Christendom one after the other introduced legalized usury, and thus got a start over the conservative nations which struggled to maintain the old moral code. To the new moral, or rather immoral, ideas thus introduced we owe the rapid development of banking in the "reformed" nations, the financial hold they acquired and maintained for three centuries. Everyone at last fell into line, and today Usury works side by side with legitimate profit, and, confused with it, has become universal throughout what used to be Christian

---

1. When I was first stammering out my elements as a boy at Oxford, a learned professor assured us in his lecture that the text of Aristotle must have become corrupt, because he could never have said so silly a thing as to call usury wrong. What St. Thomas called it I will wager he never knew.
2. I found in Tunis three years ago that the Mohammedan olive planter wanting to raise a loan for the development of his estate could not get the money from his fellow Mohammedans, but had to borrow from Europeans.

civilization. It is taken for granted that every loan shall bear interest, without inquiring whether it be productive or unproductive. The whole financial side of our civilization is still based on that false conception.

A very interesting essay might be written upon the ultimate fruits of such a conception in our own time. Were it ever written a good title for it would be, "The End of the Reign of Usury." For it is becoming pretty clear that the inherent vice of the system under which long ago the Roman Imperial social scheme broke down is beginning to break down our own international financial affairs. With this difference, however: that *they* broke down from private usury, we from public.

But that is by the way; to return to our muttons. Usury being a demand for money that is not there (a tribute levied, not upon the produce of capital, but upon a margin beyond that produce, or even upon no produce at all), Usury being therefore, when once it is universally admitted, at first a machine for ultimate draining of all wealth into the hands of lenders and for reducing the rest of the community to economic servitude at last; Usury being *at last* a system which must break down of its own weight—when the demand made is greater than all productivity can meet—why, it may be asked, has it been practiced with success for so long? Why does it seem to be at the root of so vast a progress in production throughout the world?

That it has been in use successfully for all these generations, ever since it was solidly established in general practice during the seventeenth century, no one can deny. Nor can anyone deny that it has accompanied (and, I think, been largely the cause of) the great modern expansion in production. And here arises one of those apparent contradictions between a plain mathematical truth and the results of its negation in practice, of which experience is full. Persuaded by such appearances (for they are appearances only, and deceptive), most men abandon the abstract consideration and are content with the practical result. It is on this account that even so late in the day as this the mere mention of the word "Usury" and a discussion of its ethics has about it the savor of something ridiculous.

Not so long ago everyone would have told you that to adopt the attitude I am adopting here was to write oneself down a crank. The conclusions to which every clear mind must come in the matter were not even considered, but brushed aside as imperfect notions proper to early and uncritical ages when men had not thought out economics or any other science.

The increasing, though still small number of educated men who are growing suspicious of such contempt for the immemorial past and for the moral traditions of Christendom will give these objections less weight than they were given a generation ago; but they still have overwhelming weight with the general. If you say today, "Usury is wrong," or even, "Usury is dangerous," or even no more than, "Usury must in the long run break down," all but a very few will, even today, refuse to follow this discussion of the matter. Most of the careless and all the foolish will put you into the company of those who think the earth is flat.

The error is theirs, not ours; yet their error has, as I have said, solid practical backing; for Usury has worked successfully. Productivity has been vastly increased since Usury took root. The last three hundred years have been centuries of immense expansion, and the leaders of it have been precisely those who first threw Christian morals overboard.

What is the explanation? The explanation lies in three considerations:

First, when Usury is universally permitted and enforced, it becomes only part of a general activity for the accumulation of capital with the object of investment. In the days when Usury was illegal and punished, the accumulation of capital for investment was hampered. Incidentally, those days were also days in which the production of wealth upon an increasing scale was not regarded as the end of man. But at any rate, from the purely economic point of view, the ceasing to inquire how capital would be used, the laying it down as a rule that all capital had a right to interest, no matter how it was invested, obviously tended to make accumulation more rapid, and incidentally, to make men keener to ferret out opportunities for productive as well as for unproductive lending.

With that, of course, though from other causes, went the increase of men's powers over nature, the curve of which rose more and more steeply, and perhaps is still rising—though there are signs of fatigue and of interference with that process from causes other than economic, in spite of the rapid accumulation of further scientific knowledge and of its economic application.

This increase in our powers over nature is the second reason why the false action of Usury has been masked for so long. The economic evil of Usury stimulated and accompanied great economic advantage of accumulation for Production, and this legitimate use of money had its opportunity given it by a flood of geographical discovery and new achievements in Physical Science.

The third reason why Usury has not yet worked out its full ill effect is that it has long been automatically checked by repeated breakdowns which wiped out usurious claims. Capital unproductively lent failed to receive its tribute and had to be written off. It is true that Usury on such capital is commonly the last thing to be written off;[3] but written off it is continually, and this intermittent pruning of the unearned tribute has prevented the real character of that tribute from appearing in its full force.

The nineteenth century in particular, and still more the beginning of the twentieth century, is crowded with examples of these breakdowns—myriads of them. Money is invested in a particular enterprise. The enterprise does not fulfill expectations. Though the money no longer earns legitimate interest, debentures are raised, the guaranteed interest on which is strictly Usury. For some time this interest is paid, but over and over again you find that at last even the debenture interest cannot be paid. The whole concern lapses, and the usurious tribute can no longer be exacted. You may see the process at work today in many departments of the textile industry. The mill gets into difficulties; a

---

3. Witness the continued interest still paid on bank overdrafts by our failing industries. Another excellent example of the writing off of usurious interest is the scaling down of the French and Italian debts to America.

loan is raised from the bank; interest is promised on the loan, though there is no surplus wealth over and above the cost of production. The interest is met from outside sources; but the process cannot go on forever, and there comes a time when the bank has to write the loan off as a bad debt. As the bank is making money out of other successful and profitable investments it continues to flourish, it continues to make money, its total income increases, and that part which it has lost through the breakdown of Usury is hidden in the general productive scheme; the usurious character of certain receipts is not distinguished from the legitimate character of the majority. But whenever a society shows signs of economic decay, the real nature of Usury, thus submerged and hidden in prosperous times, necessarily appears above the surface.

Mr. Orage many years ago, writing in his paper, *The New Age,* gave in this connection one of the numerous vivid illustrations of the affair, with that genius of his for exposition which ought to have made him famous. He took the example of an oasis of date-palms in the desert, the water-supply of which is got at by very primitive means. There comes a financier who lends money for development. The capital is productively used; artesian wells are sunk; the water-supply is largely increased; a better organization of the date-cultivation is begun; the produce of the oasis rapidly grows from year to year; the profits legitimately demanded by the financier are a part of the total extra annual wealth, the presence of which has been due to his enterprise. All are well-to-do; everything flourishes.

Then, whether through fatigue, or through war or pestilence, or variations in the external market, or some calamity of climate, things begin to go wrong. The annual wealth produced by the oasis declines. But the interest on the money lent must still be paid. As the cultivators get more and more embarrassed they borrow in order to pay that interest, and there comes a time of "overlap," during which, paradoxically enough, the banker appears to be more and more prosperous, though the community which supplies him is getting less and less so. But it is mere arithmetic that the process must come to an end. There will arrive a moment after which the cultivator can no longer find the money to pay the interest, which has long since ceased to be morally due. Mere coercion under an all-powerful police system has got the last penny out of him. The "overlap" between real prosperity and apparent—merely financial or paper—prosperity ceases; and the temporary wealth enjoyed by the lender comes to an end, as had previously come to an end the real prosperity of the borrower.

In other words, great banking prosperity in any particular period may be, and commonly is, the proof of all-round prosperity in that period; but it is not necessarily nor always so. The one is not an inevitable adjunct of the other.

To these general conclusions there is another objection which anyone reasonably well acquainted with history will at once make:

"You tell us" (says the objector) "that in other times when the Faith was universally held—times which you perhaps think healthier, but which were certainly much less wealthy and had to deal with, not only a simpler, but a much smaller population—Usury was forbidden. That is quite true. But when you go on to argue that there is therefore an essential difference between that time and our time, or rather the recent past which you call 'the reign of Usury,' a different ethic prevailing now from what prevailed then, you are wrong. You are confusing that which is *forbidden* with that which is *not done.* It is true that the moral code of Christendom in Catholic times forbade Usury and punished it; even as late as the *Provinciales* of Pascal men felt moral indignation against Usury, and right on to the end of the eighteenth century the punishment for Usury continued to play a part in the courts of justice and appeared in the codes of law wherever the Church had power. But in point of fact Usury has always existed, because it always must. It is impossible to draw the line between the productive and the unproductive loan. The money which I lend a sick man may so put him to rights as to make him productive again, and may therefore be regarded as indirectly a productive loan, though unproductive in original intention. The money borrowed by a spendthrift for his pleasures may, on his death, immediately after, before he has had time to waste it, pass to a thrifty heir who invests it productively. Such considerations have always worked strongly upon men's minds. That is why you find Usury plentifully existing in times and societies where it was morally condemned.

"Further, even were it possible (which surely as a rule it is not) to draw an exact line between the productive and the unproductive loan, there are all sorts of ways of evading the prohibition to take interest upon an unproductive one: to evade the duty of discovering whether the loan be productive or no. For instance, the Catholic governments, quite as much as the Protestant, issued what the French called 'Rentes'—promises made by government to pay annual incomes. Henry IV of France, after his conversion, was especially active in this form of borrowing. Philip II of Spain, the very champion of Catholicism, sank up to his neck in embarrassment due to borrowing at high interest—borrowing, by a pretty irony, from the very people who were destroying his revenue. A government going to war—that is, about to spend money in an activity commonly unproductive—begged financiers to buy of it annual claims upon the revenue; and there is no difference at all between that and the modern habit of issuing a government loan. Then there was the obvious method of signing a bond for money and receiving less than the sum mentioned in the bond. Thomas Cromwell, of pious memory, was a zealot in this practice, at a time when the full Catholic morals about Usury were still taken for granted. Much earlier, in the true Middle Ages, princes were perpetually borrowing for their wars—principally from the newly arisen Italian banking system; and earlier still, when Usury was the exceptional, but chartered and legal privilege of the Jews and a source of immense revenue to the Christian princes under whom they lived, the practice was openly admitted. Usury therefore has always gone on in human society. It always will go on; discussions upon it are academic and futile."

To this I answer that plain reasoning upon practical matters is never futile. If I say that an over-consumption of alcohol is bad for the human frame, especially in age, it is no answer to give me examples of topers who live to ninety. The evil effect of over-drinking is there, demonstrable and, to any honest mind, unquestioned. It is a mere question of experiment and experience and the use of reason applied to the same. Where true conclusions are apparently contradicted by experience they are so contradicted by other forces which do not make the truth any the less true.

So with this truth about Usury. As long as its impoverishing effects are masked or counter-balanced by stronger forces at work, they are neglected. But they are in existence all the same, and always active. To know that a truth is there, even when it is hidden, is of great practical use; such knowledge is a thing to be kept in reserve for action when the critical hour comes in which it must be applied.

Next it should be pointed out that there is all the difference in the world between a system in which an immoral principle is admitted and one in which, though the immorality is practiced, the principle is denied. There is, and presumably always will be, plenty of adultery, murder, swindling, and the rest, present in society; but the society in which the rights of property are admitted, in which marriage is sacred and to which the taking of human life is abhorrent, is very different from one where the sexes are promiscuous, or where Communism prevails, or where killing for private revenge or whim is an accepted pastime. To murder a bore, to run off with your neighbor's wife, even to pick a man's pocket, are still in our society abnormalities: abnormalities which we old-fashioned people ascribe to the Fall of Man, but which the most exuberant Pelagian will at least not deny to take place. There is all the difference in the world between a society in which such lapses continue, or are even tolerated, and one in which they are called good.

Man stands on two legs; but he can lean on one or on the other. Thus (to take an example I develop in another essay) society in the department of law must insist both upon justice and upon order; and undoubtedly in any civilized society justice tends to be sacrificed to order. But there is all the difference in the world between the atmosphere and character of a society in which injustice is held more abominable than disorder and one in which disorder is held more abominable than injustice. Two parts of one chemical element to four parts of another will give you a certain product. Change the proportions, and quite a different product appears. A society in which Usury, though practiced, is held immoral (not wholly, I admit, to the advantage of economic development) is quite a different thing from a society where Usury is held to be moral. A society in which the lender assumes it to be his moral duty to examine the object of a loan before he considers its profit to himself is different from a society in which he is not expected to do so. A world in which interest upon the unprofitable loan is detested and the Usurer is a villain is quite another society from one in which men have ceased to ask whether a loan be profitable or unprofitable; and this again is a different society from one such as ours, where interest on any loan is demanded as a sort of sacred moral right with which the productivity or lack of productivity of the loan has nothing to do.

Well, then, since to every evil there should be a remedy, what should we say about Usury today? Since I am boasting that this discussion is practical, what about practice?

Let us suppose our opponent convinced; let him make reply:

"I agree that Usury is an evil. What is more, I am inclined to agree that we are beginning to feel its evil effects throughout the world today at long last—principally through the enormous example of the great war loans. What then are we to do about it all?"

To this I answer in my turn that nothing immediate can be done. You cannot pull out a vital part of any existing social structure. The whole world today reposes upon banking, the whole system of investment renders inquiry about the productive or unproductive quality of an investment normally impossible.

There are especial private cases where you can judge the distinction clearly, and in those cases good men tend to act upon it (as in the case of loans to individuals of our private acquaintance), for the human conscience is at work all the time, even in the most corrupt and complex of societies. But in nine hundred and ninety-nine cases out of a thousand the distinction is impossible. A man is at pains to save. He must use his savings under a system where interest without examination is normal and all the infinite details of a world-wide system of production, distribution, and exchange have so long been based on the acceptation of Usury—as well as on the much larger calculation of legitimate profit—that the two can no more be divided in practice today than can the mixed colors in a dyer's vat. If I go off for six months and leave money on deposit at my bank I can hardly ask what the bank is going to do with the money; and if I did they could not tell me. No one could say how much of it goes to feeding beasts on a fur farm in Canada; how much to a young man who is getting an overdraft on his securities and spending it in riotous living; how much to the development of a useful mine in the Andes. What sane man would hesitate to put his regular little self-denials into savings certificates, or his modest £1000 into a War Loan—that crying instance of Usury? The system must go on till we break, and even the word "break" is inaccurate. If history is any guide, the true word should rather be "decay." Pleasing thought.

I did well to call this book *Essays of a Catholic* and not *Catholic Essays.* For if it became a matter of Catholic discipline that men should not today touch that unclean thing, the interest-bearing unproductive loan, discipline would stand self-condemned. The ecclesiastical order *could* not be obeyed. If by such an analysis as I am here engaged in I were to involve any of my fellow Catholics in the peculiar conclusions reached, I should be doing a very bad turn, not only to the common sense of my fellows, but to their sense of humor as well.

Nevertheless, as the scent manufacturer has it, *''Un jour viendra,''* ["A day will come"], or if you prefer Homer, ″Εσσεται ἦμαρ ὅτ᾽ ἄν. . .

It will indeed.

The Approach To The Skeptic

The skeptic is the most sympathetic to the Catholic mind of all non-Catholics: that is, if he be intelligent. For there is a Skepticism of the Intelligence as there is a Skepticism of Stupidity. The latter is intolerable. It is found in most popular works on Science, Histories of Religion, and Outlines of all kinds. But the Skepticism of the Intelligence is noble and respectable. We can present to it the claims of the Catholic Church only by admitting that its own postulates are sound, its process of reasoning accurate. We must tell intelligent Skepticism that it is on the right road, but has not gone far enough. We must ask it to appreciate. We must ask it to distinguish quality: to discover the Faith as one discovers great music or great verse.

3

THE APPROACH TO THE SKEPTIC

Skepticism may be defined as that attitude of the mind which advises us to reject any unaccustomed statement.

By "unaccustomed" I mean "That which the hearer does not happen to have acquaintance with, so that it jars with that conception of reality which he has formed through his experience."

For instance, supposing a man who died forty years ago had come to life again, and I told him I had flown through the air from Beauvais to Croydon in a machine, he would presumably doubt that statement. His doubt would be an example of Skepticism. Flying through the air in a machine was outside all the experience which he had had of earthly conditions.

In thus defining Skepticism, I do not include, of course, the larger meaning of the term, which extends it to a doubt upon one's own existence, or the existence of any reality outside one's own mind. I am talking of only what might be called "Natural Skepticism"—the twin to "Natural Religion"—the Skepticism normal to the human mind.

Again, it is not Skepticism to doubt something which is a contradiction in terms, or which is contrary to the laws of thought.

We form, by the habit of experience, a certain vague picture of reality, and that which does not conform to it we doubt. If the thing told us is too violently in contrast with our common experience, we not only doubt, we deny.

Skepticism, in the sense in which I am using the word, is eminently sane; it is native to our race, and for that matter necessary to the preservation of it and of the individual. For to accept habitually any absurd affirmation—as, that it would be safe to jump out of a fourth-story window because one was being prayed for—would lead to immediate disaster.

I insist at the outset on this natural and healthy character in human Skepticism, because it is the foundation of the thesis I desire to propose, which is this: that those who would present the truths of the Faith to those unacquainted with the process by which we come to hold them, must not only take natural Skepticism for granted, but must respect it. What is more, we of the Faith do well to safeguard in *ourselves* this robust and healthy quality; for in the absence or weakness of it we may come to accept nonsense even in sacred things, and, what is perhaps worse, we shall weaken our reasoning faculty.

Nothing does greater harm to the prestige of the Faith, to our chances of presenting it successfully to our fellow-beings, or, for that matter, to their opinion of our judgment in holding what they do not hold, than the attitude (once commoner than it now is, but still common) which denounces with a sort of horror the rejection by another of what is, to the speaker, sacred.

The horror is excusable in those to whom the negation comes as a sort of shock; those, that is, who have had no personal experience of unbelief in others; who have lived sheltered lives, and who, on hearing denied what is to them all in all, are moved to an irrational anger; but that anger is irrational all the same.

The truths propounded upon the authority of the Church consist *in part* of what we may expect any average man to accept, for they consist *in part* of truths consonant with common experience, as, for instance, the Catholic truth that right and wrong are realities, not pathetic illusions. But a great number of Catholic truths and the Catholic system as a whole, based as it is upon Mysteries and particularly upon the supreme Mystery of the Incarnation, cannot be accepted as a matter of course by those to whom it is unfamiliar. To expect them to do so—even to expect them not to be hostile—is much more unnatural on the part of one who believes than is the Skepticism of one who does not.

Now, our object in appreciating the nature of Skepticism is to combat it successfully; at least, in the things that count. Complete success in this may be called the conversion of the skeptic to Catholic truth. When we have taken the first step and appreciated the nature of Skepticism, that it is "doubt of the unaccustomed statement," we can approach the task of convincing the skeptic; but until we have taken that first step we cannot approach his conversion. It is a falsehood and a folly to tell the plain man, who has no conception of what the Faith is all about, that his rejection of its unaccustomed statements is evil. It is even wrong to call him blind. He is no more blind than a man is blind who does not see the stars by daylight.

But in our approach to the task of convincing the skeptic we must begin by distinguishing between two kinds of Skepticism, which do not merge one into the other by gradual degrees, but which are totally distinct in kind, and which may be called, the one "the Skepticism of the Intelligent," the other "the Skepticism of the Stupid."

The Skepticism of the Stupid is that denial of an unaccustomed statement which is based upon an undefined, but nonetheless real, belief that the hearer is possessed of universal knowledge. It is a common error in our day, and I touch on it elsewhere in this book.

The test of this kind of Skepticism (which, like other manifestations of stupidity, presents a formidable obstacle to human conversation) is the misuse of the word "reason."

When a man tells you that it "stands to reason" that such and such a thing, to which he is unaccustomed, *cannot* have taken place, his remark has no intellectual value whatever. Not only would he be unable to analyze his "reasons" for rejecting the statement, but he would, if pressed, be bound to give you motives based upon mere emotion. For instance, if a man tells you it "stands to reason" that a just God could not allow men to lose their souls, he suffers from the Skepticism of the Stupid.

The Skepticism proceeding from intelligence is of an exactly opposite nature.

Intelligence may be measured by the capacity of separating categories. Thus, a man who distinguishes between the office and the person is more intelligent than the man who does not. The man who distinguishes between the functions of an office in exercise and in quiescence is more intelligent than the one who does not. The man who distinguishes between the two meanings of a word often used in two senses is more intelligent than the man who does not.

For example, in the question of office. The man who confuses *infallibility* with *impeccability* is less intelligent than the man who does not; while a man who distinguishes between infallibility exercised upon a positive affirmation, and infallibility exercised in advising discretion, is more intelligent than a man who cannot so distinguish. When infallible authority bids us not to be certain on an uncertainty, it is using its function in one way. When it affirms a specific certitude it is using its function in another. A man who distinguishes between the two is more intelligent than one who does not so distinguish. Thus an authority denying the present *certitude* of man's terrestrial origin and who says "We are not fixed upon the way in which man came to be what he certainly is—quite distinct from other animals" is saying one thing. The same authority affirming the certitude of Original Sin is saying something quite different. It is right in each case, but right in a different particular. In the first statement there is not positive pronouncement on the origin of man, but only a pronouncement that, at present, this origin is not known. In the second statement there is a positive pronouncement that man suffers from a special taint incurred at the (undefined) origin of his kind. The man who sees the distinction is more intelligent than a man who mixes up the two pronouncements.

Again, in the matter of the ambiguity of words: A man who thinks that, because the Church needed "Reformation" in the early sixteenth century, therefore the disruptive movement also known as "the Reformation" was necessary and good, is less intelligent than a man who does not confuse these totally distinct terms, though they happen to be expressed by the same set of syllables.

One test of intelligence being, then, the power to separate distinct categories, the corresponding test of stupidity is inability to do so, and I say that stupid Skepticism, like stupid anything else, is the despair of the intelligent believer who tries to deal with it. He may approach it with rhetoric, or with appeals to what is the fashion, or in any other irrational way. He may even approach it with bribes. He may approach it with that very modern weapon, perpetual reiteration, after the fashion of the "slogan" upon which the masters of salesmanship depend. But all these methods are so basely unworthy of high controversy on the ultimate truths, that I would rather not contemplate them.

The approach to intelligent Skepticism is quite other. It is this: to make clear to the opposing mind what is the nature of that conviction which has settled our own minds. And in this, as it seems to me, there are three successive stages to be undertaken at the outset.

The first of these stages is to make clear what the Catholic system is. Until the elements of the unknown thing are presented, the two opposing minds are living on different planes and are reasoning from different premises.

It is not only so in this supreme matter of Catholic truth, but in any number of lesser matters. Thus, if you would persuade a man that the Humanities are of value in education, you must begin by giving him some idea of what the Humanities are. Often such a one will think that the Humanities are only a dull acquisition of languages no longer in use. If the Humanities were indeed no more than that it would be most rational to oppose such a waste of time as the acquirement of classical scholarship. Since the objector cannot see of what value the Humanities are, he must be shown by example how those who have passed through their curriculum have thereby been increased in the power of thought and of feeling, have come to the roots of our civilization, have enjoyed the highest masterpieces and have come into touch with the greatest beauty and the most profound thought; he must be shown how their experience has explained to them the European world in which they live, and perhaps may help them to save civilization, even though it has declined into its present condition.

So it is with the much greater business of the Faith. You must introduce the Person. For you must remember that in the first place the intelligent skeptic whom we approach does not, as a rule, know the full body of Catholic doctrines; and in the second place, he usually regards those which he does know (even if he is familiar with a great number) as disconnected statements not belonging to one Being, not forming a unity, not a living system spreading from a single root and inspired by a single essence, but a bundle of dead sticks.

The skeptic whom you approach must first appreciate that the Thing he is asked to examine is what it is; an organism endowed with a life, having a character and savor of its own: a personality, and, above all, a personality undoubtedly and wholly One. Next he must be shown that its judgments fit exactly to the whole range of man's being, which it at once explains, enlarges and rectifies. He must be presented with the Faith as that which demonstrably enlarges, which (in the judgment of those who hold it) undoubtedly explains, human life; which gives that life its rationale, and morally and aesthetically rectifies—that is, sanely guides and maintains in health—the same.

Not till all this has been done can you proceed to the second stage of instruction, which I take to be this: the postulating of mystery. In becoming acquainted with the Faith as the most reasonably human of things, he must also come across its mysteries—which at first he cannot accept. Your instruction must approach these and show what place they hold, what character they have; as, for instance, the Mystery of the Incarnation.

I use "instruction" in the sense, not of didactic and enforced exercises, but of the getting a man in touch with some real thing; thus, a man is instructed in seafaring by going to sea, though no formal teaching be given him; is instructed in good verse by hearing much good verse, though he be told no rules of prosody.

The Faith, I say, will be found to contain, or rather to be inextricably bound up with, mysteries. There is that supreme foundational mystery of which I have spoken, from which all flows—the doctrine of the Incarnation; and apart from the mysteries of positive intellectual doctrine, such as the mystery of the Trinity, the mystery of survival, and the rest, there are moral mysteries, nearly all of them connected with that awful double question of Will and Doom, Freedom and Fate; and there are mysteries of definition; or, again, the mystery of the Visible Church where certain superhuman powers designed for superhuman ends of holiness are necessarily exercised by human agency, often base.

Now, just as it is a test of intelligence to be able to separate categories, so it is a test of intelligence to accept mystery.

It is no test of intelligence to accept a *particular* mystery. Any number of statements could be put forth as mysteries, and all of them be false; as, for instance, the very old Puritan mystery, that there are two principles in God—the one good, the other evil. Or the highly modern mystery that evil is an illusion.

No, it is certainly not a test of intelligence to accept a *particular* mystery, but it is a test of intelligence to admit that mystery must form an inevitable part in any statement of reality. For to do so is but to acknowledge that man is limited in divers ways, and that while with one power of his mind he may see a truth, with another power another, and be certain of both, yet he may not have the further ability to reconcile the two certitudes.

A man who laughs at mystery merely because it is mystery, that is, a man who ridicules the idea that there are things beyond, but not contradictory to, our reason, may be put at once in that other category of the stupid skeptic, at whom we laugh or weep according to our mood. But the presentation of particular mysteries to the opposing skeptical mind is not the same thing as the proposing of mystery in general. The intelligent skeptic must grant you at once the existence of mystery, for he will not have passed his life without thinking, and he must have discovered that he is surrounded by mystery and is himself a mystery.

For instance, he does not exist in time immediately past nor in time immediately to come, yet he only *is* because he takes part in all three. Without extension in time a creature of time cannot be; yet what extension in time can be applied to a creature who only lives in a moment infinitesimal, and therefore in itself not extended? Or, again, what is Memory? Or again, the self-defined trinity of space, time and motion must be in one aspect static; in another aspect it is known not to be so. Or again, the mystery of personality—what is the principle of continuity therein? Is it sane to deny the oneness of personality? No. Is it sane to deny that personality is successive, perpetually disappearing into the past? No. Then what is it? And so through an indefinitely long list—all the vistas upon which the mind dwells, reaching no horizon.

The intelligent skeptic can be familiarized with the idea of mystery until it becomes a habit of his mind and takes its part, as it should, in his scheme of reality. Indeed, this second step in the approach is one certain to be reached and passed when the intelligence is sufficiently lively.

But the third step is the decisive one, and upon that all turns. Granted that the Faith is such and such; a personality with a Voice and a character; an authority whose commands and explanations can be discovered by sufficient trial to be consonant with experience; granted that the Faith's admission of mysteries is no bar to its credibility, then mystery can be accepted *if* the Church substantiates its claim to authority. Yet how shall it substantiate that claim? What proof can we bring that if there be divine authority on earth it is Hers?

Here we must approach the skeptic's last position by the presentation of that truth which our age has forgotten more than any previous age ever did—the rare knowledge that proof is of various kinds. Proof is not of one sort only; it is multiple in character. The very word "proof" takes on a different savor according to the matter towards which it is directed. Reality is reached not in one way only, as by deduction or by measurement, or by observation, or by the elimination of possible alternatives, but in any one of each of these ways, or by two or more combined, or by any one of an indefinite number of other ways, each specially applicable to the indefinite number of problems presented.

Would you prove to a man that two sides of a triangle are longer than the third, you may go through the deductive mathematical proof; but if you would prove to him that Jones has not committed a particular murder, you must enter into the field of known human motives, and of known human capacities; man being known not to have the power of bilocation, you may establish an alibi, or you may prove the absence of motive. Would you prove that Swift is a better writer than Kipling, you cannot establish certainty in the same degree; but in your efforts to convince anyone who doubted such a proposition your methods would probably be to make him familiar with numerous parallel examples taken from these two masters. Would you prove that the music of Mozart more charms the ear than the siren of a steamboat, you would appeal to repeated experience of the two sounds; in morals you would appeal to the moral sense; in beauty to the aesthetic; as in physical science to measurement, coupled with the postulate that things happening repeatedly in the same fashion presumably follow a process normally invariable. In every case your proof must vary with the nature of the thesis to be proved.

Now, I have said that the chief difficulty before us today, in presenting the proof of the Faith, is that appeals to mathematical science or to experimental physical science are almost the only kinds to which men are *now* directed by their education. Lack of use has atrophied what should be the common powers of mankind in other fields; powers taken for granted in a better past.

Those powers, in presenting the Faith to the intelligent skeptic, we must seek to revive, for the intellectual basis of the Faith is not that of positive proof, using the word "positive" in the scientific or mathematical sense; but an appeal to proof within one category: that applicable to Holiness. If there be Holiness on earth, what institution is Holy? One only: The Faith. The Faith is witness to itself. It is a proof by taste. If the quality be perceived, it is unmistakable; conviction follows. If it be not perceived, there is no other avenue. For the sense is of grace; the acceptation an act of the will. The Faith, I say, is witness to itself. The Faith convinces of its truth by its holiness; is its own witness to its own holiness, whereby also it is known. There is much more: there is its consonance with external and historical reality upon every side; there is personal experience, gained by living it, of its consonance with reality in daily detail, of its wisdom in judgment, of its harmonies where human character and the effect of action are concerned; of its perfect proportions, which are such that all within that system is in tune with all, and each part with the whole. And there is further this: that the Faith is unique; it is not one among many kinds of similar things. It is not *a* religion amongst many religions. It is like the I AM of Holy Writ, from which it also proceeds.

All that. All that. I do not say that you will thus convince; but I say it is by this progression that the intelligent skeptic, our only worthy opponent, can at last be brought into the household.

First to know where the House is: then to be shown that the gates are open. Then to find himself in the House. And what other roof is there in this world?

THE CATHOLIC CHURCH AND THE MODERN STATE

The thesis that the Catholic Church is incompatible with the Modern State is in part true. Three fundamental reasons are urged to show this incompatibility. The first—that the Catholic section of a state claims the right to destroy all religious bodies in disagreement with it—is unsound, being based on a misconception which can only arise from an ignorance both of Catholic doctrine and of the history of Catholic peoples.

But the other two reasons given are sound: one is that obedience to an external authority is contrary to that ideal of citizenship, which in the Modern State is based upon two ideas—that each citizen individually forms his decision and that a majority of these decisions binds all; the other is that the claims of the Church tend to conflict with the similar claims of the modern laical, absolute State. Hitherto the truth of these two reasons has been masked by the fact that the bulk of Catholic moral teaching has been retained in non-Catholic states. But this is changing, and conflict will result.

4

THE CATHOLIC CHURCH AND THE MODERN STATE

This essay is written in reply to one recently published in the United States of America, which supported the familiar thesis that the Catholic Church is incompatible with the Modern State; that the Modern State holds a doctrine of sovereignty such that the Catholic Church cannot be fully accommodated therewith, and such that a conflict necessarily arises.

The thesis is *in part* true. I am not concerned here to deny it as a whole, but to examine it; to see in what points the argument advanced shows knowledge of the Church's claims, in what they are misunderstood.

As I write in reference to an American article and as these lines will be read as much in America as in England, I must make due allowance for the special conditions of the American political system; but for the rest I think the debate applies to any sovereign country of the modern type.

I need hardly add that I attach no moral value to the word "modern." It only means "contemporary" and is mortal as other forms have been. I deal, then, with the Modern State not as with something having any unquestioned merit, such that anything unsuited to it is thereby condemned, but as only one of many forms of society which probably will not last much longer but which, while it lasts, the Catholic must consider. It may be called the "Electoral State" reposing on what are called liberal theories of government.

Let us first of all define the issue.

It is not a general issue, but one limited to terms of reference as opposed to which I here reply.

I find opposed to me three fundamental objections to any harmonious relation between the Church and the Modern State. These are:

(1) That the claims of the Catholic Church to a universal right of judgment in faith and morals include both in theory and in practice the claim to destroy, by any means, other conflicting bodies in disagreement with it (pagans, schismatics, heretics). Therefore the Modern State, meaning thereby a State which is not officially Catholic—that is, not one in which Catholicism and citizenship are equivalent—stands in peril from the presence in its midst of a Catholic body. For that body, though but a part, must, by the nature of its claims and character, arrogate to itself the right of destroying the rest.

(2) That the subjection of the reason made by Catholics to a general authority outside the individual, and in particular to Papal authority, is incompatible with citizenship in the Modern State. For that citizenship is based upon two conceptions: *(a)* That all questions whatsoever must be decided by each citizen individually in complete freedom from any authority; *(b)* That such decisions being collected, a majority of them binds the minority to obedience.

(3) That the claims of the Catholic Church being universal, tend to conflict with the claims of the modern laical, absolute State, which are particular. Perhaps my opponents will quarrel with my using the terms "laical" and "absolute." "Laical" I can defend as meaning the conception that the Modern State is not allowed by its principles to adopt or support any one defined and named transcendental philosophy or religion. On this point I think all will agree with me.

The Modern Electoral State does indeed always and inevitably support one general religious attitude and oppress its opposite very strongly, but by implication only, and indirectly; it would be shocked if it were accused of doing even that; and a defined and named religion it does not and, consistently, cannot openly adopt.

As for the word "absolute," I do not use it in the sense of "absolute government," but in the sense that the Modern Civil State, like the old Pagan Civil State of antiquity (to which it is so rapidly approaching in type), will brook no division of sovereignty. Its citizens are required by it to give allegiance to the State *alone,* and to no external power whatsoever. I think my opponents will also agree with me in this sense of the word "absolute." The Modern State differs from the Medieval State in that it claims complete independence from all authority other than its own, whereas the Medieval State regarded itself as only part of Christendom and bound by the general morals and arrangements of Christian men. This absolutism of the Modern State began in the sixteenth century with the affirmation of the Protestant princes that their power was not responsible to Christendom or its officers, but independent of them. It had its immediate fruit in what was called "The Divine Right of Kings," whereof the claim of a modern government, whether monarchical, republican or whatnot, to undivided allegiance is the heir.

Now, of these three fundamental objections I wholly disagree with the first, and find it based on a misconception. The fear that Catholics will, or should, work otherwise than by persuasion for the destruction of an established non-Catholic society around them can only arise from an ignorance of history and of Catholic doctrine.

With the second I disagree partly, and partly agree. I agree that if there were, or could be, a citizenship based on the supposed independence of the individual from moral law and a State ruled in all things by majorities of citizens, each of whom should vote according to his private decision on any matter, Catholics could not give implicit obedience to so strange a commonwealth. On the other hand, I disagree with this objection if it means that the normal duties of citizens (as we know them to be in practice) cannot be discharged in full by Catholics. The history of Catholics living within a non-Catholic State shows this, and the philosophy held by Catholics upon civic duties will make them, if they are good Catholics, better citizens, *saving Catholic morals,* than any others. For they alone will be able to give ultimate reasons for obedience to the laws, whether in a State upon the Democratic model (as in Andorra), the Oligarchic (as in England and all Parliamentary countries), or the Monarchic (as in Italy).

As to the third proposition, I find myself wholly in agreement with it. In my judgment a conflict between the State claiming unlimited powers and the Catholic Church is inevitable. Whether the State be "Modern" or no, seems to me quite indifferent. Whether it be Democratic—as some small States can be; Oligarchic—as are all States dependent on elected bodies; or Monarchic—governed by one president or king, elected, imposed, or hereditary—the Civil State is always potentially in conflict with the Catholic Church. And when the Civil State claims absolute authority for its laws in all matters, then it will inevitably come sooner or later into active conflict with the Catholic Church.

Now let me deal with the first point—the only one in which I wholly disagree with the thesis: the idea that Catholics as individuals and as a body cannot but attempt to destroy by other means than persuasion whatever is non-Catholic in the State to which they owe allegiance.

I say that, as to this first point, I disagree. The fear that a Catholic body within a non-Catholic society will use all means to destroy the non-Catholic elements in the society around it and to reduce it by force or fraud to the Catholic discipline is baseless. The Catholic body will not so act; and its abstention will not proceed from fear, but from the nature of its own principles. It is true that as these principles by definition assert the truth and goodness of Catholic doctrine they necessarily imply the falsity and evil of anti-Catholic doctrine. It is true that a Catholic regards heretical and Pagan morals as things which do harm and which any society would be well rid of. But it does not follow that the Catholic will therefore act directly for the destruction of the evil by other means than conversion. And the reason should be clear. It is, that in any system no one fundamental principle works alone, but all have to work in accordance with others. In this case the Principle that the Church is possessed of Truth and that dissent from Truth produces evil which should be eliminated, has to work in accordance with another Principle, that of Justice.

A Catholic society is amply justified by all Catholic Principles in fighting the beginnings of disruption within its own body; it is amply justified in making Catholic ideas and education, manners and all the rest of it the rule within a Catholic State. It is amply justified in struggling long and hard—as Catholic Christendom did for more than a century after 1521—to prevent the break-up of a founded Catholic society such as Europe had been for many hundred years, and to save the unity of its civilization. But it is not justified *by its own principles* in so attacking a non-Catholic society already long established and traditional, because that society possesses rights—for instance, the right of the family to train the child—aggression against which would offend justice.

A Pagan society where the Church is a newcomer, a Protestant society where the Church forms but one particular body, alien in spirit to the rest, a Modern society becoming Pagan (as ours now is), in the midst of which the Church so finds herself, is certainly to be affected by Catholic efforts at conversion. Catholics always have and always will attempt to transform the society around them by that process, wherein they may succeed, as in the case of the Roman Empire, or fail as (hitherto) in the case of the Japanese; but this effort at converting a society traditionally anti-Catholic bears no relation to the forcible action justly and rightly exercised within a Catholic society in its own defense. A Catholic nation, a Catholic civilization, has a good right to check by force what proposes to destroy it: just as the State based on ownership has a right to check by force communism or theft. But a Catholic body in an anti-Catholic society has no right to attack that society. The two cases are not only not parallel, they are contradictory. For instance, if I can by force or fraud prevent a Mormon child today from joining his family and so being brought up Mormon, and if I exercise that force or fraud I am doing wrong. But if, in a monogamous State, I attempt by arms to prevent Mormonism, at its inception, from introducing Polygamy into a Monogamous society, I am doing right.

The distinction is simple and should be clear, but I see that an argument is found to the contrary in the recent Concordat between the Church and the Italian State.

This Concordat excludes from certain civil functions (notably teaching in State schools) unfrocked priests. It recognizes the Catholic Church as the State religion of Italy, giving no other ecclesiastical corporation or body of opinion that same position. It gives the Catholic Church entry into, and its doctrines a permanent position in, public education. This, it is said, shows what Catholic intention is in changing the constitutional law of the State. The contention is that the Catholic Church claims and would exercise tyrannical powers over large and established non-Catholic bodies within the State where it had power. Whether it be the action of a majority or no is indifferent. The point is that it is tyrannical.

Now, it is remarked by our opponents that the claims of the Catholic Church extend "over the whole world." It is further remarked that, according to those claims, there is "no parity between Catholic and other religions"; that, "moral and educational authority" (as exercised by the Church) "are identified with the authority of God Himself," whence it is concluded that all dissidence therefrom, on whatever scale and from whatever source, would be treated by Catholics as an enemy is treated, actively, and its suppression attempted by force. In the same way there is quoted the definition on heresy, the punishment and the extirpation thereof. It is remarked that "disobedience to the Pope is affirmed to be morally wrong": (the idea that such dissidence necessarily involves damnation shows ignorance of the Catholic doctrine on the nature of salvation and its attainment). The conclusion is drawn in a sentence which seems to me to sum up the position. It is this, that *"Catholic claims,"* it is said, *"submit the sovereignty of the State to the supremacy of the Catholic Church."* If for "submit" we read "except from," and for "the supremacy" we read "the moral laws and doctrine," I regard that sentence as accurate.

But these changes in wording are essential, and with regard to the whole of this point the answer is simple enough.

It is indeed inevitable that any corporation claiming to be what the Catholic Church claims to be, to wit, the only Divine authority on earth in matters of faith and morals, shall by theory claim universal jurisdiction in these; but it is not true that this jurisdiction either is in practice or should be in justice, exercised as it is here imagined it would be. There is neither a conspiracy so to exercise it nor a desire so to exercise it; and the very examples given are proofs of this. The essential of action against heresy is that it takes place for the purpose of checking the inception and growth of something foreign to, and destructive of, Catholic society. The laws against heresy in Catholic societies of the past, the struggle against heresy during the great religious wars of from three to four hundred years ago, were both of that nature. As against an established, permanent, large non-Catholic body there is no such attitude.

If you doubt it, look at the attitude of the Church towards the Jews. Here, if anywhere, there should have been, according to this erroneous theory of Catholic action, a policy of extermination. The Jewish community should have been forbidden to exist; its children should have been taken from it and brought up in the Catholic Faith wholesale; its worship should have been forbidden; it should have been the subject of a crusade. History is a flat contradiction of this. Alien and unpopular, the subject of violent mob attacks, treated as foreigners by the civil power, and therefore liable to expulsion, the Jewish body, when the Church was at the height of its power in Europe, was specially protected in its privileges so far as moral theology could protect it. When Jews conspired against the State or were thought to be so conspiring, as in Spain, the State persecuted them. But there never was, and there never will be, an effort made by the Catholic Church as such to absorb or destroy that hostile community by force. The same is true of an established heretical body, or for that matter of an established Pagan body. I mean by "established," forming a large and well-rooted corporation within the State, composed of myriads who are in good faith, and living a settled traditional life of its own, reposing upon long-secured foundations. It is perfectly true that the civil power will always tend to extrude what it regards as alien and hostile; but Catholic moral theology as such has never countenanced action against those bodies only because their faith and morals were not in full harmony with the Catholic Church.

What does happen, and naturally happen, is that where the whole code of a society is Catholic, laws and institutions will follow that code, and the recent Italian Concordat is a very good example of this. The Catholics in Italy are not a political majority any more than English-speakers in the United States are a political majority. Italy is *organically* Catholic, not mechanically. She is a Catholic country, not an arrangement of voters drawn up by party machines into Catholic and non-Catholic. She is a Catholic realm, in the same sense in which the Massachusetts of the Colonial period was a Puritan colony, or Japan is a Pagan empire today. It is normal in a country Catholic to the roots that an unfrocked priest should not be allowed to teach (public opinion alone, apart from laws, would see to that!), that education should be upon Catholic lines, and that the Catholic Church should be the established Church of the realm. The arrangements which apply to such conditions have no parallel in a community where those conditions do not exist.

But all this is not connected with mere majorities. In all this misconception, perhaps the gravest and yet the most characteristic is the idea that a "Catholic majority" in the modern political sense of that word would impose Catholicism over the "minority" standing against it. The whole idea is wildly wrong. Such an idea as the Divine right of mechanical majorities has no place in Catholic philosophy. It is one machinery of government. It is being widely questioned in Europe, though still preserving an uncertain life in some States. It may be right or wrong. But, anyhow, a Catholic majority would never, in Catholic eyes—unless it was so large as to be organically identical with the general tone of society (which is a very different thing from a mechanical majority)—give sufficient sanction for action against those who dissented from it.

So much for the first point; the imaginary peril which a Protestant or Pagan society is supposed to run from the force or fraud of Catholicism in its midst. That Catholicism in its midst is an alien thing is perfectly true. That men should dread its moral influence as something which disintegrates that Protestantism or Paganism which is the soul of their society is natural and inevitable. That they should proceed to regard it as a conspiracy against them capable of aggressive action is extravagant and out of touch with reality.

As to the second point, that the Church produces a citizen other than that conceived as the ideal citizen of the Modern Electoral Liberal State, I agree.

According to definition the ideal citizen of this Modern State must be free to act on his individual judgment of morals, must reach conclusions on all matters by that private judgment, but must accept the coercion of any law whatsoever when it has been decided by a majority of such individual citizens so concluding. For instance, of a hundred citizens in such a State, forty-nine, each thinking it out for himself, decide that each may, without moral wrong, eat beef; fifty-one decide that beef is unholy and must not be eaten. The fifty-one may morally coerce the forty-nine and forbid them beef (or beer, or coffee or whatever it may be).

It is pointed out with perfect accuracy that the Catholic does not decide moral questions in this manner. The Catholic belief in the authoritative claims of the Catholic Church to define morals prevents that. It is further pointed out with justice that the individual Catholic accepts as superior to his own judgment the judgment of the Church, and in certain cases the judgment of the Papacy, on the conception that the Pope is the Vicar of Christ on earth. But there is in the general non-Catholic conception of what this attitude means one essential error. The error consists in the idea that the Catholic attitude is irrational or non-rational while the attitude of the non-Catholic is rational. The contrast is not of this sort.

All men accept authority. The difference between different groups lies in the type of authority which they accept. The Catholic has arrived at the conviction, or, if you will, has been given and has retained the conviction (some come in from outside; some go outside and come back again; most receive the Faith by instruction in youth, but test it in maturity by experience) that there has been a Divine revelation. He discovers or recognizes a special action of God upon this earth over and above that general action which all who are not atheists admit. He discovers or recognizes a certain personality and voice—that of the Catholic Church—which conforms to the necessary marks of holiness and right proportion, and the ramification of doctrine from which is both consistent and wholly good. The incarnation of the Deity in the Man Jesus Christ, the immortality of the human soul, its responsibility to its Creator for good and evil done in this world, its consequent fate after death, the main rite and doctrine of the Eucharist—these and a host of other affirmations are not dissociated, but form a consistent whole, which is not only the sole full guide to right living in this world, but the sole just group of affirmations upon the nature of things.

To take up that position is to be a Catholic. To doubt it or deny it is to oppose Catholicism.

But that position is taken up under the fierce light of reason. It is indeed puerile to imagine that it could be taken up under any other light. A proposition so awful and so singular is not accepted blindfold; it is of its very nature subject to instant inquiry. It is not a thing to be taken for granted, as are ideals which all accept as a matter of course. On the contrary, it is of its very nature exceptional, unlikely, and not only requires examination before it can be accepted, but an act of the will. Nor is it true, as men ignorant of history pretend, that in barbaric and uncritical times (of which they think the Faith a survival) these truths were accepted without inspection, and that the argument from reason is a modern one. Throughout the ages from the first apologetic of the Church in the second century to the present day, without interruption throughout the Dark Ages and later throughout the Middle, and all through the high intellectual life of the sixteenth, seventeenth, and eighteenth centuries, the appeal to reason by Catholics has been universal and continuous. Today, in the twentieth century, Catholics are the *only* organized body consistently appealing to the reason and to the immutable laws of thought as against the *a priori* conceptions of physical scientists and the muddled emotionalism of ephemeral philosophic systems.

It is my own experience, and I think that of most Catholics who have mixed much with opponents of their religion, that nowhere outside the household of the Faith is the speculative reason fully active and completely free, save possibly, as a rare exception, in a few of the more intelligent skeptics. The Catholic may perhaps accept such a man as Huxley for an intellectual equal in this appeal to the reason. But he accepts very few non-Catholics as his intellectual equals. He cannot but note that, in the vast majority, non-Catholics accept their authority without inquiry. It is, for the bulk of them, a mixture of what they happen to have read, of common daily experience (which boggles at all mysteries and marvels), and running through it all is a pseudo-scientific attitude not far removed from materialism, which they have none of them analyzed and which only appears by perpetual implication: as when they presume without attempt at proof that what they call "natural law" is unalterable, or when they fall back upon a name or a book or "the latest criticism" in the place of argument.

So much for that. The Catholic acts upon reason when he recognizes goodness, holiness, and the authoritative Divine character in the Church, just as a man acts upon reason when he recognizes an individual voice or face.

Having accepted such authority, reason demands imperatively the subjection of one's own less perfect experience and less perfect power. I can arrive by my reason and by my experience of the world at a certitude that the Catholic Church is the sole Divine authority upon earth. I cannot arrive by my reason at a certitude that man's obviously corrupt nature can obtain eternal beatitude. My reason can only accept that at second-hand from authority. I meet a professional politician fresh from his last piece of villainy: blackmail or bribery, or other corruption. Certainly it is not my *reason* that tells me such a creature is a candidate for eternal bliss. I am constrained to believe it on the Authority of the Faith.

A parallel instance (though an imperfect one) is the map. When we take a government survey and accept its authority there follows as a secondary consequence our acceptation of a particular point upon it, as that this town is north of that river, though we have no personal experience in the matter. I say that the parallel is imperfect, because no one, I hope, would give to a surveyor or any other human instrument the authority attaching to Divine revelation.

But though the Catholic bases his Faith upon Reason, that Faith, once held, certainly prevents him from playing the part assigned to the ideal citizen of the Modern State. Neither will he submit all things to separate and individual private judgment, nor will he necessarily and always obey as a moral duty laws arrived at by the mechanical process of majorities. On a multitude of things—e.g., the nature and obligations of marriage—he will accept established doctrine and prefer it to any possible conclusions of his own limited experience, judgment and powers. Should a majority order him to act against Catholic morals (as, for instance, by a law compelling the limitation of families) he would refuse to obey it. It is equally true that if in some grave point of Faith or Morals not yet defined the Papacy decided Catholic morals to involve resistance to a new law, the Catholic would resist that law. For instance, suppose a majority to order for all young children of the Modern State a certain course of instruction in certain sexual matters. The matter is subjected to individual judgment. Some are for, some against. At last it is solemnly and publicly promulgated from Rome that the proposed instruction violates Catholic morals. Then Catholics would thenceforward resist the decision of the majority and refuse to submit their children to such instruction in the State schools.

Incidentally, I may say that the position of the Papacy is misunderstood when it is regarded as a despotic authority acting capriciously. It is part and parcel of the Catholic Church, defining and guiding—not inventing—doctrine, and identified with the general life of Catholicism. Catholics act as they do, not because one individual has taken into his head to give them orders on a sudden, but because they are in tune with the whole spirit of the Catholic Church, of which the Pope is the central authority.

As an example of the misunderstanding, I may quote the attitude often taken by Non-Catholics towards the advice given by Leo XIII and subsequent Popes in the matter of Scholastic Philosophy. "Pius X," we are told, "ordained that a philosophy which flourished in the thirteenth century should be the philosophy of the twentieth," and this attitude is compared to that of an American fundamentalist denying the conclusions of geology. All that is out of focus. No such thing was ever "ordained." Cardinal Mercier's great revival of scholasticism at Louvain was approved and commended, and its study warmly supported. But no Catholic is bound to accept that particular system or its terms. I may say in passing that anyone who does adopt it seems to me wise, for it derives from Aristotle, the tutor of the human race, and it represents the highest intellectual effort ever made by man; nor is there conflict between it and evidence, nor any reason to believe that our own particularly muddled time with its disuse of reason is philosophically superior merely because it comes last. But scholasticism is only a human system of thought; it is not of revelation; and the idea that it could be thought equivalent to the Faith or that the Papacy was here imposing it as of Faith could only occur to one wholly unfamiliar with the ancient and abiding Religion of Christendom.

The Papacy directs in a great number of disciplinary matters, as of liturgy, ecclesiastical law, etc., which do not normally touch civil life. On those rare and grave occasions when it acts with plenary and doctrinal authority it says nothing new. It defines and promulgates a truth always possessed.

However, whether from the general authority of the Church, her spirit, traditions, annals or definitions, or from the particular authority of the Pope, it remains true that the Catholic cannot be an ideal citizen of the Modern State as defined above. He cannot pledge himself blindfold to accept any and every decision of a mere majority. He must envisage the possibility of such a decision traversing the divine Law, and he will not (as does the Ideal Citizen of the Modern State) regard all subjects whatsoever as matters for private judgment changeable and reversible at will; for some subjects are to him of their nature fixed and changeless.

From this it will be seen that on the third point I am wholly in agreement. If there is ground for conflict between Catholicism and the ideal of the citizen in the Modern State, still more is there, *and has always been,* ground for conflict between the Church and any form of Civil State which regards itself as absolute: and that conflict may appear, in a future perhaps not very remote.

I have already said that a non-Catholic may quarrel with my use of the word "absolute," and indeed there is a danger of ambiguity in that term. It may be pointed out that the Modern Electoral State is not "absolute" in the sense of "arbitrary." Its power proceeds in a certain limited fashion according to a certain guiding machinery; but it *is* absolute in the sense that it admits no other authority than its own, in whatever province it chooses to exercise that authority. And this claim of the Modern State to absolute authority is the more remarkable because the Modern State is but one of many. It is not a universal state; it only exists in a restricted area, has only existed for a short time, may not endure even where it is today most blindly accepted, and yet it acts as though it had complete, unlimited and eternal rights over the soul of man.

The old Pagan Roman Empire in its war with Catholicism did at least claim to be universal, and its original quarrel with the Catholic Church, of which all the first three centuries are full, was due to a conflict between two universal authorities.

Each Modern State is but one among many rivals; yet does it claim greater powers than ever the State claimed before, and with those powers I submit that the Catholic Church must inevitably come into conflict sooner or later; not because the State is modern, but because it claims unquestioned authority in all things.

I notice, for instance, that certain of our critics are particularly shocked by the admirable statement issued on the part of the English Catholic bishops just before the late General Election in Britain, where they say that it is no part of the State's duty to teach, and add that *authority over the child belongs not to the State, but to the parent.* Nothing could be more odious in the ears of modern Nationalism—because nothing is more true. In the face of this tremendous claim of the Modern State, a claim which not even the Roman Empire made, the right to teach what it wills to every child in the community, that is, to form the whole mind of the nation on its own despotic fiat—our critics cannot maintain that the Modern State does not pretend to be "absolute." It is in fact more absolute than any Pagan state of the past ever was. What is more, its absoluteness increases daily; that is why its conflict with Catholicism seems to be inevitable.

The issue is very well stated when abhorrence is expressed (by implication) of a recent authoritative Catholic pronouncement, that "if certain laws are declared invalid by the Catholic Church, they are not binding." Here, as we have just seen, is the whole point. Where there is a conflict between civil law and the moral law of the Catholic Church, members of the Catholic Church will resist the civil law and obey the law of the Church. And when this happens you get that active dissension between the Church and the State which history records in all the great persecutions. That was the very crux between the Roman Empire and the Catholic Church before Constantine. In the eyes of the civil power the Christians were rebels; in the eyes of the Christians the civil power was commanding practices which no Catholic could adopt. It was demanding duties which no Catholic could admit.

That the quarrel has not yet broken out into open form (save here and there in the shape of a few riots) is due to the fact that *hitherto* the bulk of Catholic doctrines have been retained in States of non-Catholic culture. But as the moral distance grows greater between the Catholic and the non-Catholic, as the Modern State reverts more and more to that Paganism which is the natural end of those who abandon Catholicism, the direct contrast cannot fail to pass from the realm of theory to that of practice.

It is inevitable there should appear in any Absolute State, not alone in States which still trust to the machinery of voting, but in all States, Monarchic or Democratic, Plutocratic or Communist, laws which no Catholic will obey. One or two tentative efforts have already been made at such laws. When those laws are presented to Catholics there will at once arise the situation which has arisen successively time and again for nearly two thousand years; the refusal on the part of Catholics, which refusal in the eyes of the State is rebellion. There will follow upon that what the State calls the punishment of disobedience, and what Catholics have always called, and will once again call, persecution. It will be accompanied by considerable apostasy, but also considerable heroism; and in the upshot the Faith's power to survive will lie in this: that devotion to the Faith is stronger, more rational, better founded, more tenacious, more lasting in substance, than that hatred which the Faith also, and naturally, arouses.

The Conversion Of England

The conversion of England would seem impossible of attainment. If it is to be attained it can only be attained by recognizing the nature of the obstacles to it, much the strongest of which is the patriotism of the English people; the Faith is in their eyes alien and therefore something inferior as well as something to be hated. Approach through the gentry is no longer possible, for the gentry have ceased to govern; our efforts must be upon the bulk, the chaotic masses of town population. Such small chance as it has lies in two forms of action—exposing the insufficiency and absurdity of the official anti-Catholic history and philosophy—that is, undermining the opponent—and, on the positive side, creating a fashion in favor of the Faith, or at any rate of sympathy with the Faith.

5

THE CONVERSION OF ENGLAND

I

Humanly speaking, it is impossible.

I do not say impossible in a thousand years, after I know not what transformations and catastrophes, when our civilization shall have broken down, as every civilization does in its turn, and when men shall have been taught reality by chastisement. But humanly speaking, it is impossible.

It was difficult enough apparently in our fathers' time; they thought it at least possible, however, and they showed their wisdom in concentrating upon it; for in the conversion of England one main problem of civilization would be solved. It was the defection of England from the Faith that made the break-up of Europe possible (for without the gradual uprooting of the Faith in England Europe would have remained one, instead of falling into the chaos which it presents today) so the restoration of England, while England is still powerful, would probably lead at last to the reunion of Europe.

But humanly speaking, it is impossible.

It is impossible within the limits of, say, a couple of centuries. It is impossible for the effects of the change to be observable within, say, seventy years. I give those figures, "seventy years," "two hundred years," because they are the figures of the original process in the time when the vested interest of rich men and the patient genius of the Cecils gradually crushed out the Faith of the English people. It was a process covering nearly two hundred years from first to last (1525-1715), and a process of which the main effects began to be apparent after about seventy years of governmental effort (1530-40; 1600-10).

Now, if we are to examine the conditions of a task apparently impossible, our first business is to inquire why it should seem beyond our powers. One can deal with no problem until one has analyzed its nature. What is the nature of the resistance presented by England to perceiving once again what was manifest to all Englishmen when England was in the making, and from returning home to that which was the native air of England for eight hundred years? The obstacle lies in the present character of the English people and in four salient manifestations of that character. These four salient characteristics are the English imaginative power, rendering Englishmen strongly emotional and also strongly attached to national myths; the English patriotism, which is by this time fixedly associated with anti-Catholic ideas; English homogeneity, which makes England present a solid block of hostility to Catholicism and presents no considerable dissentient body upon which Catholic influence could begin; and English self-sufficiency, which makes Englishmen certain that what they are, to wit, anti-Catholic, is necessarily superior to what they might be. Of these four the first was not the product of the Reformation, the second was enhanced by the Reformation, the last two are the special creations of Protestantism.

Of the strong English emotionalism and imaginative power working today in anti-Catholic social tradition and habit, in other words the anti-Catholic character of the English polity, here are certain examples:

No one will deny that for a sentiment of indignation against the maltreatment of animals the English are distinguished. In their vehemence on this point they stand out from all other nations, and particularly from the Catholic nations. The feeling is due to strong imaginative power and emotionalism. Its excess is clearly at issue with Catholic culture. We all know this, both from the ridicule and anger it excites among foreigners of a Catholic culture and from the corresponding intensity of reproach which is levied by Englishmen against, let us say, the Italians in their management of animals. The Catholic takes the affair in a different proportion from the anti-Catholic, whether that anti-Catholic be Buddhist or Protestant.

For instance, I read in my newspaper that a man in a small way of business in a suburb, trying to get rid of a cat which was diseased, and failing to do so by poison, knocked it on the head several times until it was killed. For this action he was condemned to prison, his life presumably ruined and his human home destroyed, on the evidence of a person paid to discover such cases by a private society. On reading the report of this, your average Englishman would say: "Serves him right. The cat and the man are both of them part of animated creation, not different essentially; there is less difference between a man and what are called the higher animals than between these and the lower forms of life. Animals have rights just as we have..." and so on. All that way of looking at such things is the product of intense imagination and emotionalism working on a false philosophy.

To men of Catholic culture this mixing up of men and animals in one category is not only false, but abominable. The report of such a case in Catholic social surroundings would raise a storm. The destruction of a human home for the sake of a cat would seem intolerable. As for animals having rights, the Catholic system of morals specifically denies that. We have duties to God in regard to animals, but they have no duties to us. There is no contract between us; and they are made for our service.

Here is only one example, but a forcible one, and I think the concrete instance is illuminating.

The Englishman instinctively feels that a change in religion, that is, in his philosophy of life, would change him on this point where his emotions and imagination are deeply engaged. He feels in his bones that if his people fell to accepting in the bulk the atmosphere of Catholicism, his peculiar sympathy with the beasts would be lessened. And he is quite right. It is an example of the way in which the high emotional and imaginative power of the Englishman, captured by an anti-Catholic philosophy, is today a force against Catholicism.

Now consider another effect of this vivid imaginative power

of England, captured as it has been, and now at the service of anti-Catholicism: I mean the myths and legends of England as she is today. The historical story taught to Englishmen and forming part of their general education in the schools, in the universities, through fiction, through the press, through conversation, is one strong body of national myth all on the anti-Catholic side. The historical heroes, not only national but foreign, are the anti-Catholic heroes—William the Silent, the great Cecil, the corsairs of the Reformation, with Drake at their head, Henry of Navarre, Gustavus Adolphus—and so on through a hundred names. While upon the other side stand the villains—Philip II of Spain, Louis XIV, James II, Torquemada, Mary Tudor, and the whole list of the Catholic champions.

Exceptions are granted for the sake of emphasis, but in every case of these exceptions—from Sir Thomas More to Saint Francis of Assisi—what is praised is not the specifically Catholic thing about them, but what they have in common with the Protestant ethic: in the case of More the heroic defense of a private conviction; in the case of Saint Francis a general tenderness to the natural life around him. But who can conceive the modern Englishman devoted to Saint Dominic, the great twin saint to Saint Francis and historically an equal figure? The governmental attempt to stamp out the revolution under Mary Tudor is put forward as an exceptional horror, anti-national in character and abominable; a corresponding and successful attempt—successful because it lasted over a much longer space of time and was much more universally applied—to extirpate the Mass by torture, mutilation, exile and terror in every form, is represented as a national achievement. The reign of the Cecils, the period 1559-1606, over which this effort was spread and in which it triumphed, is the chief national legend, apparent in every book and enshrined in the noblest verse.

In all this, I say, you find the vivid, creative imagination of the English—the power which sends them out on adventures, that fills their literature with landscape, that has given the world its highest treasure of lyric verse: for the English lyric, manifold, intense, vast in volume, is supreme.

As for patriotism, that second character in the English which renders the task of conversion, as I have called it, impossible, why, English patriotism is best defined in the phrase—"Patriotism is the religion of the English." In no other society is the worship of the corporate body of the nation exalted to such a height, and this worship of the native country as an idol—which was the great moral force whereby Cecil worked his religious revolution under Elizabeth—is the main cause of English Homogeneity. Such a religion of nationalism demands the close cohesion of the national character, which is the very object of its adoration. It would be impossible in England to imagine those divisions which have affected other nations, such as the French or the Irish. One cannot imagine in England armed conflict between two political theories struggling to the death as they have recently struggled in Ireland. One cannot imagine in England a Dreyfus case, with its upshot in the deliberate ruin of the national army by one faction and the resultant of the Great War. There has not been civil conflict in England (save of the wealthy against popular monarchy) since England became the modern and Protestant country it is. It is always when you touch the patriotic nerve in Englishmen that you are at serious issue with them, for in asking England to be other than she is you are asking whom you address to be renegades from their religion—that religion of patriotism.

That, I say, has helped England to become, beyond any other nation, all of one stuff; and this solidarity, this unity, opposes in a block all prospect of essential change. This character is rightly recognized by Englishmen as the peculiar strength of their state. To whatever strain social relations may be put, unity is preserved. But there was another factor at work: aristocracy.

The political instrument whereby this striking homogeneity in the English social structure was attained was aristocracy. It was under the rule of the gentry, now in jeopardy, or rather manifestly declining, that the unity of the English thing was brought into being; and this aristocratic constitution of the English world was, in its turn, a direct result of the Reformation, which killed popular monarchy by enriching the squires with the loot of the Church and making them and their great working committee, Parliament, the master and supplanter of the Crown.

This unity is of especial effect on foreign policy. It has been the making of the English Imperial power. It may also be observed in the absence of all active criticism against public men, and in the absence of any real political opposition—indeed, for Englishmen, the very word "opposition" in politics has come to mean a label in a rather dull game. Of internal opposition—such as Rome, France, Ireland, have thrived on—the English remember no more than did Venice in the sixteenth century.

The effect of this unity may, again, be seen in the spontaneous discipline observed by the Press, and even by men in general conversation, whereby that which it is agreed not to mention, never is. Citizens of other nations, accustomed to full discussion of public affairs and to mortal struggle between contrary policies, marvel at the result. They do well to marvel, for it is unique in the world. This homogeneity, like the preceding characteristics we have noticed, stands firm against all efforts at disintegration: all effort at changing one part of the whole; yet one part must be changed before the whole can be changed. With an effort at the conversion of England there would soon come a stage where that effort meant differentiation between one part of the nation and the other.

Take another example of this unity: the passion for order, because disorder threatens unity. In the English polity the effect of law is directed towards the preservation of order as its prime end.

Now, the law and its courts, its magistrates and its officers have in every society whatsoever two causes to serve. These two causes are Justice and Order. In heaven the two are coincident. On earth they are in practice convergent, but not identical. You must in practice lean either towards the side of Justice or towards the side of Order. In the Catholic atmosphere the emphasis is on Justice, in the anti-Catholic it is upon Order. In both, every effort is made by good men to combine the two, but when the one must be sacrificed to the other or when there must be compromise between them to the advantage of the one or the other, the Catholic ethic results in an emphasis upon Justice, the anti-Catholic in an emphasis upon Order. And this is more strikingly seen in the English system of administration and legal judgment than in any other of the more modern nations. The English system is the supreme example of an emphasis upon Order; and by that system England has secured a more perfect social security and a more exact machinery of administration than any other country. Disorder abroad is the laughingstock of the English. Exactitude of rule in the taking of evidence, for instance, precision and definition therein, are native to the English system; laxity or elasticity in this matter abroad is for Englishmen a constant source of amusement and, on the rare occasions when they are themselves subject to it, of exasperation.

Yet when England was Catholic the courts obtained the name which they still preserve. They were called "Courts of Justice," not "Courts of Order."

Nothing is commoner than to hear in England today an interesting conversation between lawyers upon why a man was condemned, although he may well have been innocent. He committed this technical error; his counsel played the game badly in this or that respect. Nothing is more typical of the social attitude adopted than the half ironic but very serious phrase: "After all, if a policeman is attacked somebody ought to be hanged." And talking of hanging, what a gulf between the old phrase which is still retained as a fossil, "malice prepense," in the definition of murder, compared with actual practice, in this non-Catholic society! "Malice prepense" signifies a desire to do some evil act, entertained before that act was accomplished and guiding the act to its conclusion. A man who slowly poisons another is guilty of "malice prepense." The phrase is retained from other times, but it no longer has vitality. A burglar who shoots at a man in order to escape and kills that man is held guilty of murder, though he had no intention of killing him, but only of wounding him. Save in very exceptional cases, passionate crime, which is certainly not premeditated, is treated as murder. Why? Because it is thought all-important to prevent the killing of citizens by other citizens, and, with that end made preponderant, England is rendered freer from such killing than any other State of similar magnitude and complexity. On this freedom from disorder Englishmen universally congratulate themselves and are often congratulated by foreigners, and it is an excellent proof that order has precedence over justice. From the same source we obtain the celerity of English law, and particularly of English criminal law, in its action; and that immense power of the police which is so much greater in England than the corresponding power of their fellows in any other nation.

Here, then, also, you have that passion for political unity at work; and such English unity, the very mark of the English political soul today, would be directly menaced by the first serious expansion of Catholicism within the realm.

Even the small Catholic body already existing is a cause of misgiving, though that body is so gentle and apologetic that its power is not seriously considered. Let it become stronger, let the English instinct for solidarity be threatened, and the society around us will react most vigorously against the Church.

Lastly, there is that indurated quality which those who would give it a bad name (as I would) call "self-sufficiency" and those who would give it a good name call "a just recognition of our own superiority." This is not peculiar to England; it is a mark of all the Protestant culture.

It is very genuine, and so profoundly rooted today that it coexists with the very being of the nation. Such a spirit is held without question to be a strength; the notion of humility is either not grasped at all or, when glimpsed, is felt at once to be a weakness.

This sense of superiority is nourished in the simplest but most effective fashion by an unconscious permanent insistence upon what is well done in one's own society, and an ignoring or ignorance of what is done ill. Instinctively, when comparison is made between one's own people and another, those things wherein we excel are treated as the tests of universal excellence. Those things wherein we fall behind others are either not noticed or treated as unimportant.

The sense of superiority here spoken of is nowadays of a piece with all the rest. It supports as it proceeds from homogeneity and patriotism and is fed and sustained by the vigorous imagination of the race. The man from Huddersfield, walking in Siena, notices Dagoes. The man from—let us say, Rugby—remarks that Napoleon was not a gentleman. So powerful is the work of fancy here that men tell you how deeply foreigners admire them and praise those foreigners for showing such good sense.

You feel this national sense of superiority very strongly in the contrasting spheres of administration and government. Mechanical administration being better carried out here than elsewhere, foreign societies are tested by their success or failure to reach a similar standard in mechanical administration. In the efficiency of the police, of the secret intelligence service, of the civil service (notably in the Post Office), English administration is supreme. Government—which, when we are governing aliens means the molding of men's minds towards our own fashion and is a success or failure according to whether we can stamp them with our own character or fail to do so—is felt to be unimportant. Why Rome and Spain did these things, why France is doing them today, Englishmen do not trouble to inquire. They only note that in the department of administration—to which we usually give the name (wrongly) of government—the rivals of England do not approach her standards. She is unrivalled therein.

Of this sense of superiority, appearing in a thousand ways, I will give two concluding examples, taken among thousands—the phrase: "We are not a logical nation," and the sincere affectation of national virtue. The phrase: "We are not a logical nation" is perpetually used as a term of praise, with not a shadow of suspicion that it may equally be a confession of imbecility. The reiterated sentences in which men congratulate themselves upon some common virtue as peculiarly their nation's own, have the same source. Some few of these expressions are disappearing; for instance, one does not often hear, as a commonplace, allusions to the purity of Parliamentary life or the Spartan indifference to money among politicians; the absence of all financial scandals at Westminster. But there has been no attempt at stopping corruption—for that would be an admission that it existed. Instead of criticism, or what would be much better, punishment, there is silence; and this silence is the best proof you could have of how strong is the feeling of which I speak.

Well, that feeling of superiority, like all the other characteristics I have here considered, works permanently and effectively against such a metamorphosis from the anti-Catholic to the Catholic, as the phrase "Conversion of England" implies.

The Reformers were very proud of translating the word *μετανοια* [*metanoia*] in the New Testament by the word "repentance," and were never weary of denouncing the old Catholic translation, "doing penance." But the old Catholic translation is the best, for to do penance is an active change, and unless you *do* penance you have not really undergone a change at all. And in their weaker word to express the older stronger word they have managed to get rid altogether of the thing for which the word stood; the reformers have made repentance, humanly speaking, impossible.

II

Well, then, to begin again, the Conversion of England is impossible.

But nothing is impossible with God, save things which are contrary to His nature.

What is more, things which seem, humanly speaking, impossible, are discovered in the course of no very long lifetime to take place all the same.

I have myself seen in the course of forty active years not a few impossibilities take place. I have seen the boundary between the gentry of England and the classes inferior to them grow very indistinct, and the gentry selling themselves in case after case to men whom, a lifetime ago, they would have treated as untouchables.

I have seen England, with its very small professional army and with military operations on any large scale unknown to it within the memory of man, produce suddenly a force of two millions fully equipped and increasing in value with miraculous rapidity, though trained on the very field of action.

I have seen what may appear the most remarkable example of all, the disappearance from the most humorous nation in the world of most of the old popular humor, the disappearance of all funny papers (of the sheet, for instance, which published the Bab Ballads), of the old music-halls and of the glorious old popular comic songs. If a thing like that can happen in the social order on a minor scale—not of the very first import, though significant—it would seem to be possible in a higher order. Now, the order wherein this desired achievement, the Conversion of England, should take place, is the highest order possible; and it is precisely on that highest level that the incredible becomes credible and the impossible possible. Those who have seen, as we have all seen, individual conversions by the score which were, humanly speaking, inconceivable, cannot call even so great an operation as the Conversion of England impossible.

If that be so—and it is so—let us consider in what direction effort would seem to offer most prospect of fruit.

III

We must consider a new method, because the old method has failed. By which I do not mean it has failed to convert England—it has obviously failed to do that—but it is not even going forward. It is actually in retrogression. And we must consider why it failed, in order to understand what new method now proposes itself to us. For the choice of a right method in any effort is by a process of elimination.

The old methods depended upon the social state in which England stood when they were first so enthusiastically proposed and when they were thought by many to have such great and even immediate chances of success. Some eighty years ago, the days of Newman's and Manning's reconciliation with the Faith, the Conversion of England was envisaged by the small but enthusiastic Catholic body of that time upon lines consonant to social structure. The agreement between action and environment was not wholy conscious, of course. In most men it was not, perhaps, conscious at all. It was taken for granted as part of the air they breathed.

They were themselves citizens of a country ruled by a select governing class. It was a country in which all, or nearly all, rulers and ruled, were steeped in a doctrinal atmosphere, a social atmosphere wherein nearly all men and women accepted certain main Christian doctrines. The converts among them (who were the leaders in the effort at general conversion) had come out of that atmosphere; they were familiar with it; it seemed to them an inevitable concomitant of English life as they knew it.

Today all that has changed. A transmutation of English thought cannot come today through the old channels. It cannot spread from something socially superior to what lies below; and, more important, the doctrinal atmosphere has evaporated. Outside the Catholic body few now believe in the main doctrines.

Let us first see what the old method was.

An upper class in those days was, I say, everything. The Press which "counted" was the Press which catered for the educated and the leisured; even the daily papers, though the cultured affected to despise them, were manifestly not written for the mass of Englishmen, and, indeed, the mass of Englishmen did not generally read at all. (I am not falling into the silly error that the mass of the older England was less cultivated than the mass of England today—it was far more cultivated, as any one of us can testify who remembers the older generation of the poor. But the habit of reading was not widespread as it is today, and, above all, it was not constant and repetitive as it is today). There were in those days drawing-rooms, which some even tried to pronounce after the French fashion and call "salons," and even those who like neither the native nor the foreign term will admit that there were receptions and converse of the gentry wherein opinion was formed and from which it seeped downwards, percolating through the structure of the nation. In such commerce political ideas were nourished and developed. In the surroundings and furniture of a leisured class religious ideas also were nourished and developed. The university was an expression of that upper class. The intellectual domination exercised by the university was a class domination; and in the universities, especially at Oxford, the battle of religion raged. Everyone was familiar with the issue, and to the majority which opposed there stood up a very brilliant, advancing, minority which supported this or that element in Catholic tradition.

Meanwhile, all the body upon which attempted conversion had to work, the stuff of England, was as I have said, *doctrinal.* The ancient and fundamental Catholic doctrines were possessed by all, or by so nearly all as made no difference. The tone of English life was doctrinal. The conception of personal immortality, our responsibility for good and evil, the presence of a personal, just and good God, the Creator and Judge of us all, these main Catholic doctrines were still fundamentally English, expressed English ideas, and resulted in English conduct. There was a Heaven and there was a Hell, however much one might wrangle about Purgatory. The great bulk of English men and women, moreover, accepted the idea of the Incarnation, not as a tradition to be clung to, nor as a memory, but as a truth which formed part of the body of thought. Skepticism had its place in that same leisured class which gave its tone to the whole, but it had very little place amid the run of the people.

Now, there was in all this a certain factor of social structure too much forgotten today and important for us to insist upon when we envisage the difference between those times and ours. England was agricultural; and England remained agricultural on through the greater part of Queen Victoria's reign. The England of forty-five to fifty years ago which I can remember as a boy was an England the older members of which, the still living men and women who decently trained their children, and who still bore witness to their own traditions, had been born in the villages. Most of them already lived in the great industrial towns, but they had known other things and had been formed under other influences. Even to this day the life of the English village, insofar as it survives (it is now the environment of a petty minority), is possessed of the old traditions of thought and in great measure of the conduct following upon those traditions—

which traditions may generally be called by the vague term, Christian. The villagers were organized under squires. The leisured class, the cultivated, ruled ideas even more than they did things, because they were the natural and present heads of village communities into which the bulk of people had been born.

A host of consequences followed upon this agricultural origin of Englishmen. For one thing, they were in touch with reality as people always are who live upon the soil. They were in touch with organized religion; the village had its calendar, and though its feasts were few it knew its feasts. The village church was a center, and the village clergyman, who then was much more of one class than he is today, led intellectually. The fine parsonages in which it is so difficult for the impoverished modern clergy to carry on, witness to that past. The Englishman of the village, the Englishman born in the village, getting his strong impressions of childhood there, though he were early absorbed by the industrial centers, the modern great cities, was trained to individual impressions. The people with authority over him were people he knew, his neighbors were real neighbors, there was upon him the pressure of society, and that society was organized—it was not as are our millions of the city now, an inchoate dust.

Things standing thus, the Conversion of England seemed within my own memory to be a question of change in leading individuals, of spreading the idea of the Church among those who typified ideas and fed upon them.

Notable individual conversions among the gentry and intellectuals thus pointed towards the conversion of the nation. Not only the numbers of such conversions, which were at one moment considerable, but much more their character, impressed the people of the time. There was certainly a phase during this development in which it seemed reasonable to believe that though the efforts were made against great odds the effort might succeed. We should recover an appreciable section of the gentry and their example would spread. It was not put in so many words; it was not seen, even by the most enthusiastic, for what it was; but therein lay the soul of the effort. Every new name added to the roll call heartened those who had put before them that distant goal, difficult, yet not apparently impossible, of attainment. Through the movement in the universities, through the movement in the English Church, through the movement in the great households, through the movement among what some foreigners call the "intelligentsia," the thing was going forward.

I have used with regard to all this the brutal term "failure." I have said that the thing failed; and though the term is brutal it is exact. The tradition so founded was strong and continued to run in a full stream on into our own time, but it did not spread. We all know what happened; and there were two factors in that happening.

The first factor was this. What was morally the major part of the affair, the tendency, was captured by nationalism, "patriotism—the religion of the English." "I will not leave the Church of my baptism."

There arose the historical theory generally called "continuity." There arose as a consequence with many what is also called "the branch theory." Catholic ideas spread, not only within the organization of the established Church—where they became very powerful—but outside its boundaries; and in our own time there have been most striking effects of this in certain of the Nonconformist [non-Anglican Protestant] bodies; also (what is in my eyes most remarkable) in the general attitude of skeptics towards history and towards contemporary thought. Many who had no faith at all grew to be in sympathy with some one aspect of Catholicism, and sometimes with many aspects. But the major tenet of Catholicism from which it both derives its name and spiritually lives—*that the Church as one thing is separate from all that is not the Church*—struck no root. That vital point—the Church divine, all else man-made—did not affect those who were thus impressed among Anglicans, skeptics, and even the Non-conformist bodies by much else in Catholicism. The reason that this essential tenet of a Divine Supremacy in the Church failed to catch hold was the necessary conflict between that tenet and the worship of the State, which is also the love of the Nation. Catholicism seemed the more alien the more vigorously it acted; the more it showed its intellectual and moral strength the more un-English was its savor.

The second factor in the failure was the social transformation of England. The Englishman ceased to be a country-man and became what was once, and perhaps still is, called at Oxford a "townee"—I apologize for the term, but it is short and convenient. A generation was born and grew up which had never known anything but the great modern city. The influences of the modern city molded the character first of an enlarging majority and lastly of nearly all the nation.

I would not be so foolish as to ascribe the vast business of modern English change to one such cause; there were many others. The gentry left all for money; yet, at the same time, great wealth became unstable, so the town masses went adrift without leadership. At the same time, the fact that physical science was achieving its triumphs so rapidly, and upon so steep a curve of progression, happened to be accompanied by a process which has nothing to do with physical science as such, but which colored the whole of its influence, a process in which its votaries and leaders became in bulk the active enemies of defined and organized religion and specifically of Christian doctrine. The idea of the miraculous, and its concomitant, the sacramental idea, became inconceivable to those few who analyzed and thought; negligible and forgotten to those who did not.

When the sacramental idea and miracles are presented to the modern Englishman in the bulk he finds them so contemptible that he cannot believe them to be seriously held; or, if held, held only through an illusion which a little instruction will dissipate. To such a base intellectual level have the masses fallen!

But of all the causes I still think that the most prominent, if not the most profound, is the transformation of England from an agricultural to an urban society: and urban not in the organic sense of a city inspiring its citizens, but urban in the sense of that mere loose sand, that formless mass, of our town millions. They all must read trash, and read it continually; they are all formed upon a state system of "education" (as it is called—for the term is most misleading) which is compulsory and universal, and which has for one of its main products the modern Press of England. I mean by the word "Press" the newspapers which are in every hand and the flood of popular fiction, the accepted official view of history—especially of national history—and all the other forms of lamentable ignorance which proceed from this source, including the increasing ignorance of Europe and of what was once meant by Christendom.

Now, upon *that* urban body the old method and the old tradition have no grasp. To the attention of *those* millions the old path by which it was imagined that the Conversion of England might be reached does not lead.

This truth can be tested numerically. Individual conversions seem more notable than ever, or, at any rate, more notable than they were in the intervening period, after the first great burst of Catholic effort more than a lifetime ago. But in proportion to the population our numbers do not increase, or, if they increase, increase but slowly. And what is more, the "penumbra"—the belt of non-Catholic sympathizers with Catholicism—does not extend, but, on the contrary has shrunk; so that there is now a fairly definite line to be drawn between the well-lit world of active Catholicism, and the dark anti-Catholic world outside.

The time when travel, instructed, curious, based upon high culture, worked in our favor has ended. There is indefinitely more travel than there was, but it is deaf, blind and of no cultural effect. The time when historical reading worked through the cultivated and the leisured, the time when Lingard was the chief historian of England (he was the first to write our history soundly, to base it upon numerous documents; he was the founder of modern English history and he is still—though now never acknowledged—the principal source of it) has concluded. That chapter has come to an end.

Note further that there is within the Catholic body itself a noticeable result of the new state of affairs. The non-Catholic attitude has for now some considerable time past affected the Catholic body. We have not molded the university to our own image, it has molded us. Our historical textbooks, those upon which our Catholic youth is trained, are the textbooks of the opposition. When the Church is fighting her battle in some foreign land the English Catholic does not know what is toward; if he sees her in peril he foolishly falls into the nationalist error of congratulating himself that this particular kind of peril is not felt by himself; and in practice, though he would be horrified to hear it, he is singing the old refrain which thanks God for having made him a Happy English Child.

I have found this very marked in the matter of the Religious Orders. Where they are persecuted and exiled it is due to the natural depravity of foreigners—in our blessed island world no such injustice would be tolerated. The magnitude of the struggle between the Church and the world is altogether missed by us. Conversely, millions upon millions of Catholics throughout the world who are maintaining the Faith have ceased to trouble themselves upon the lack of sympathy felt for them by the handful of Catholics here. During the close wrestling which we called the Irish question, and which was essentially a religious struggle, we know how leading Catholic opinion stood in England and how much of it was contemptuous of the Irish claim. All England, you may say, was ignorant of the great force arrayed against it across St. George's Channel, but none were more completely wrong in their calculation of that force than the small group of English Catholics, who thought of it only in terms of nationality. No one was more bewildered by the result, when Catholic Ireland recently achieved her partial, but very considerable, success. It is, I think, indubitable that the conversion of England through an upper class and through the organs which the upper class used to control, is no longer to be considered.

The old method has failed. Upon what new lines are we to advance?

IV

The new method should begin with an appreciation of the main *new* factors in the problem. Some of the old factors remain, notably the profound feeling throughout England that Catholicism is alien and anti-national. But the new factors are what we must especially seize. These we have seen. They are the change of England from an aristocratic state to a state we know not what as yet, but certainly less and less aristocratic; a body of millions which have the town habit, are under the town influences, molded by a Press with whose character we are only too familiar, and now cut off from all the older agricultural traditions of England. We shall no longer achieve our purpose through the gentry; we shall no longer advance it through the infiltration of what is a rapidly dwindling and less and less effectual cultivated class.

The next point in the modern situation, arising out of this first one, is the omnipresence of the State in England today, particularly in the field of instruction. This State influence is uniform, intensely national, and in all its spirit less and less Christian.

The third factor, equally allied to the other two, is the spread of a mood which is already that of the greatest number and may soon be that of all England outside the little Catholic body. This mood is contemptuous of tradition in religion, has quite forgotten doctrine and has come to think all dogmatic definition absurd.

The first conclusion to be drawn, I think, in the presence of this new problem and of the new factors of which it is composed, is that two new efforts must be made, apart from, and supplementary to, the effort at individual conversion.

One of these efforts is negative, the perpetual criticism and ridicule of and attack upon the indurated, half-consciously held, but strongly anti-Catholic, philosophy of the world against which we are moving. The other is positive. We must instruct, not in the sense of instructing the individual, but in the sense of giving the new great town masses a general idea, at least, of what the Church is.

But here I would digress upon that phrase "supplementary to" individual conversions.

It is in the nature of the thing that the advance of the Catholic Church, now as at all other times, must be effected, ultimately, by individual conversions; so was the Church originally founded, so did it recover what it had lost in the sixteenth century, and, indeed, conversion can never be anything but individual by definition; to call it anything else *in its essence* would be a contradiction in terms. The process of individual conversions will be the constant and inevitable process of Catholicism wherever it has sufficient vitality to advance at all. There is not, in any new method, room for slackening here; the appeal to the individual, the revelation of reality to the individual, remains the cell and unit of effort. If that were not present, no mass effect could develop. But I say that "supplementary to it" must be a new conception of the way in which we should set to work, and I say that that new conception involves the two directives of negation against what is false, and of instructing the mass, the bulk; of making the idea of the Church familiar.

The first of these directives, the negation of what is false, is the easier mechanically, but morally far the more difficult of the two. To undermine the crude false philosophy opposed to us, to loosen its hold on the masses by ridicule of its ignorance, exposure of its errors, satire of its pompous self-assurance and isolation, is a task open to any man. The method is easily available. But it involves very unpleasant consequences to the agent. We need such agents, nonetheless. Without them we shall do nothing. As it seems to me (and Heaven knows that here I am being more personal than ever and present myself as a target for abuse) we need Tertullians. We must be militant. There were, perhaps, in the past, moments when that spirit was unwise; today, it seems to me demanded by a just judgment of the situation. Our society has become a mob. The mob loves a scrap, and it is right. We must attack the enemy in his form of rationalistic "science," we must analyze and expose his hidden false postulates, so that the individuals who hold those postulates shall be brought to shame—but to bring a man to shame makes him angry. His anger, I think, is a test of our success.

We must expose the confusion of thought in the opposing camp; its ignorance of the world and of the past, its absurd idols. And in doing so we must face, not only ideas—which is easy—but men, the defenders of those ideas—which is difficult. We must wound and destroy.

Such action involves suffering. Now, there is no lack of

heroism, God knows, in the effort made by each individual convert to advance the Faith against the mountainous forces opposed to it. The individual convert suffers here in England as he suffers nowhere else. The body of English converts is a body everywhere heroical. I know not one of them, even among the rich, who has not shown heroism nor one who has not faced extremes of suffering from loss of fortune, loss of close ties in friendship and blood, loss, above all, of that support which a man feels when he is in tune with society around him and with his own past.

But here is a call for suffering of a new kind. There is (as I take it) today a necessity for braving *corporate* opinion, and those who get on horseback to challenge that particular dragon are in for a very bad time. You will be despised or disapproved if you practice your religion quietly with no effort to oppose its organized enemies, but if you overtly attack these enemies you will get something much worse than disapproval. Every weapon will be turned against the man who is attempting to destroy the defenses thrown up against us.

Boycott is the strongest of those weapons and the most effective; he will have to endure that. Where the boycott cannot be applied he will have to endure the reputation of a crank, of an absurdity. He will become an "object." Whatever irrelevant truth or falsehood can be dragged in against him will appear. The more plainly he speaks the more will he be accused of paradox. The stronger his appreciation of the national past the more will he be accused of foreign taste. He will lose fame and repute, he will quite certainly suffer in his pocket, he will lose affection. Remember that the reaction of men against what they dislike is exactly proportioned to its activity. Now, activity is the condition of success. When the great Lord Salisbury said (I believe I am quoting him rightly though only from memory): "First find out what particularly annoys your enemy and then do it as often as ever you can," he was proposing a sound rule of combat. That is the spirit in which victories are achieved. Nor is it blameworthy. On the contrary, it is glorious. It is indeed blameworthy to attack with the mere object of irritation, it is also futile and vulgar; but to challenge active hate as the proper means to a good end—that is excellent.

Thus, if you wish to undermine the false authority of false history, it is not enough to expose particular misconceptions which have arisen from some ignorance of detail in the matter of Faith; if the man is an enemy of the Faith, then let his whole body of work be battered. Let him be fallen upon. Let it be argued from his bad judgment in particular affairs that his judgment in the main affair is also bad. If there is a lack of good faith in his method let that be proved, not only by examples pertinent to religion, but also by examples which have nothing to do with the main quarrel in themselves, but which are pertinent to the general thesis that the enemies of the chief truth are the enemies of all truth. . . So may the siege be joined, and those engaged in it will be surprised to discover the wealth of ammunition prepared to meet them. When all else is exhausted there remains this most perilous of all perils menacing those who attack to undermine: calumny. That also must be faced. The attacker of corporate opinion will be a target for calumny.

As for those who maintain that militancy is barren, I will reply with the precisely contrary truth, that conflict is the mother of all things. The most powerful ally one can have is fashion, and fashion is set when a battle is won. But a battle is not won without wounds.

The first signs of victory (if the impossible victory be achieved) will be, I say, a change in fashion. Long before we have made it fashionable to be Catholic we may have made it fashionable to sympathize with Catholicism. Long before we have made it fashionable to sympathize with Catholicism, we may have made it fashionable to ridicule anti-Catholic history, anti-Catholic materialism, anti-Catholic morals.

Fashion is a tawdry ally—but we must not despise it. Fashion governs with peculiar power in times such as ours when intelligence is failing. And fashion is set by the energetic few.

The second directive, the positive one, is instruction. I have said that it is the easier morally, and so it is, by far; but mechanically it is the harder. You do not excite enmity by merely making the nature of a system known. The most violent enemy of Socialism would be interested in reading a book which explains what it is. The most ruthless invader is ready for maps of the enemy's country. The moral side of instruction is easy, for there are no risks to be run and nothing to suffer but boredom. The mechanical side of it, the method of achieving it, is hard to obtain. Merely to formulate fact is easy. But *how* to get instruction "over the footlights," *how* to get the elements of Catholicism known to the urban masses is a difficult question to answer. One thing, however, is certain, we must here act in general upon society. In other words, our advance must be political.

I do not use the word "political" in the ridiculous sense of that puppet show, the professional politics of the House of Commons. *There* action has no value, sincerity or meaning, even in temporal things, such as the economic struggle, still less in the majestic warfare of the Church. The idea of a Catholic party, now that the word "party" means nothing, would in England be ridiculous; and whether a Catholic votes for this or that empty label, "labor" or "liberal," in the dreary business of an election is of no consequence whatsoever. Our votes mean today nothing, save in the matter of the schools.

Should there arise tomorrow a considerable party of politicians labelled "Communist," I can see no reason why a Catholic should not vote for the worthy Mr. Jones, who wants to increase his income as a lawyer or as a company promoter by getting into Parliament under the title "Communist," quite as innocently as for the worthy Mr. Brown, his cousin, who wants to achieve exactly the same ends in the card-shuffling game under any other label—"Patriot," for instance. Neither the presence of Mr. Brown or Mr. Jones among the dull herd of the House of Commons will make any difference to England. It is not the House of Commons that governs nowadays. I can easily imagine in the future a Catholic saying to his fellow Catholic: "Are you voting Patriot or Communist this time?" just as he said a few years ago, "Are you voting Unionist?"—meaning, are you voting for the people who will be nominally in conduct of affairs when the real financial masters of the country decide to destroy the union with Ireland.

No, I mean "political" in the true sense. An effort is political when it aims at changing the structure of society, and in that sense must we work to instruct and to use the result of our instruction. We must act upon the masses as citizens, through the means by which the masses are today reached.

It is advice more easily given than applied. What methods are available to us at the outset of our efforts? What are available to a small body possessing at the outset none of the engines for popular appeal? There are two kinds of methods: the direct and the indirect. The direct offers the least opportunity; the indirect, the greatest.

Not the cinema, certainly. Not, as yet, the schools; for the schools are controlled by the State, and, from the elementary schools to the university, are based on anti-Catholic history, philosophy and everything else.

There is the platform. The work done by the Catholic Evidence Guild is an example. Such a method has the greatest of traditions behind it, for by preaching and exposition of this kind was the Church founded throughout Europe in the great missionary time of the fourth, fifth and sixth centuries. And in this we have once more on our side the energy of the Irish.

What of the Press in this province? I would here emit an opinion purely personal and repeated at greater length on later pages of this volume; I do not think that instruction is to be achieved mainly by the serial Press. I am nearly certain that it cannot be achieved by a daily Press; I think it is to be achieved mainly by books. But insofar as we can act through a serial Press, the weekly journal is the strongest force, and the prime condition of it must be an economic guarantee. We should subsidize in order to make certain of the effort in that field.

Though no action through social leadership is possible, action through intellectual leadership is still doubtfully possible; a good review, read by non-Catholics, would, I think, ultimately affect opinion.

But the best way to use the Press for instruction is by challenge: by repeatedly asking, and occasionally obtaining, space in the popular journals, *where we are read by non-Catholics,* to correct false impressions. By telling the truth in such free-lance work, in letters, in reported speeches, in protests upon Catholic countries, the Catholic past, the nature of Catholic doctrines. The great need here is industry: repetition. We are working up hill. Our chief danger is fatigue.

Again, while we lack the machinery for popular dissemination of truth, yet if we make that dissemination our aim its effect will appear. Most of us do the opposite. Most of us are careful to keep out of quarrels. If all of us, or the greater part of us, few though we are, kept protest and statement continually alive, *some* corporate effect would follow.

The indirect method is far the most promising. Every day practical problems arise, every day the difficulties of our dissolving civilization are brought up sharply against the daily lives of our fellows. The breakdown of marriage, of property, of Christian morals as a whole in modern England has come rapidly upon us, and whenever the acute necessity for a solution arises *we* can be there with the solution. We might end, if our effort here be untiring, by making men associate the Faith—of which now they as yet know nothing—with the remedy for their immediate ills.

For we should always remember this, perhaps the only consoling thing one can remember in the desperate and difficult situation of the Faith here in England today: that in the very negations around us lies our opportunity.

We alone have the key to the lock; we alone have the cypher of life; we alone are in full touch with reality; we alone are the organized and certain definers of morals; we alone can throw the chaos into order and give perspective and proportion to the torturing confusion in which men find themselves throughout the modern world, and particularly where it is at issue with the Catholic Church.

Sooner or later every man asks himself the Great Questions. No man can of himself discover the replies to them. We alone have the replies. These replies form one consistent body of thought, each part supporting each, and all in company building up one grand reply wherein alone the human spirit can repose.

Though the need for satisfaction is universal it does not follow that men will turn to the source from whence alone it can proceed, but, at any rate, they will find no other. We gamble on that chance; we stake upon that opportunity. Those around us, for whose recovery we set out, are in despair, or, at any rate, will, each of them, at some time come up against despair. We alone can present the solvent to despair. And such men as come to know that the claim is made will not neglect it.

The Counter-attack Through History

Ever since the Reformation, the attack on the Faith has been principally conducted on the field of history. The defense against this attack has been mismanaged, untenable positions have been held too long, and through many defeats there has grown up a weak defensive spirit which can never achieve results. The time has come for us to take the counter-offensive; for, with the expansion of historical knowledge, history is now with us. Truth confirms truth.

6

THE COUNTER-ATTACK THROUGH HISTORY

I ought, perhaps, to have called this essay "The Apologetic from History." I prefer the more provocative title, because it is the more true. There is a permanent general need for an apologetic drawn from history; but there is particular need, urgent at the present moment, for a counter-attack upon the false history which has been used to undermine the Catholic Faith in the minds of men, to shake the confidence of Catholics in themselves, or to confirm in error those who are brought up in error.

The Apologetic for the Faith is theological of its nature. Historical argument is but subsidiary to theological argument where the Faith is concerned; just as the defense of geometrical truth must be mathematical in nature, and appeals to its truth through experiment can only be subsidiary to the mathematical proof. You must have a mathematical proof to show that the square on the hypotenuse is equal to the squares on the other two sides; and if you illustrate this truth by giving practical examples these are but supports to your main principle.

Those who spread the Catholic Faith throughout the world did not as a rule depend upon historical arguments, nor perhaps shall we have to depend upon them in a later and better condition than that of today. If we are in this time of ours especially concerned with the historical argument, it is because the historical argument has been used against us with such violence and so successfully. We have suffered for over four hundred years an attack which was mainly an appeal to history; to repel that attack we must undertake the counter-offensive; and the moment is highly propitious for so salutary and inspiring an exercise.

When the attack upon the Church began (I mean the main modern attack, for attacks in various forms have never ceased since Herod's deplorable panic) it was of necessity an attack historical. And for this reason, that the Church was, in the moment of the great rebellion against it in the early part of the sixteenth century, most vulnerable upon the historical side. Even those (and they were at first a great majority) who had no malice against essential doctrine, but were genuinely keen upon rightful reformation, were necessarily moved by the appeal to history; and it goes without saying that if men like the Blessed Thomas More were thus moved, those who desired the destruction of the Church rather than its reformation exulted in the historical argument.

The historical argument was of such force four hundred years ago for two reasons: first, the Church suffered from an accretion of myth; second—and this is most important—the getting rid of myth involved an appeal to an earlier state of affairs before the myth had arisen. Once that appeal to an earlier state of affairs was familiar, there arose a fatally easy association of ideas between the appeal to primitive times because they were free from error, and the appeal to primitive times simply because they were primitive. In the same way you may say to a man who has grown slothful in middle age: "Remember the example of your energetic youth!"—then, when you have made a sort of idol of this youthful period, you may persuade him to exercise quite unfitted to his present age; and so kill him. An honest reformer would point out that the supposed relics of a saint were spurious, and perhaps would prove it; he would then enlarge upon the exaggeration of devotion to these relics—for nearly every good habit can suffer from exaggeration; he would then be in a mood to dilate upon the undoubted truth that the reverence shown to this saint had grown with the years, and thence to note the historical fact—equally true—that in the very first years of the Church, relics had not the importance they came to have later. At last he might be led, if he were muddle-headed, to the absurd conclusion that one ought not to venerate relics at all. Or he would discover some perfectly sound doctrine to be abused by the exaggeration of enthusiasts; for instance, the doctrine that Papal power may dispense from other than Divine law, could be—and was by more than one excited supporter—made to cover cases which most undoubtedly *did* come under Divine law, and cases, therefore, where there was no Papal power of dispensation. The reformer, moved by this abuse, would show that the power of dispensation had developed in scope; would go on to remark that in its original form the definition of this doctrine was less detailed than in its later form. From this it would be easy, by a natural confusion of mind, to begin arguing that the original nebulous form of the doctrine of dispensation, when it had not yet been abused, *must* be preferable to the later developed form of the doctrine, when it had been abused, and at last the reformer would be occupied in getting the very earliest statements he could find, giving them moral value in the order of their priority.

When the upheaval took place in the first generation of the sixteenth century, when it occupied the minds of nearly all men who had been born between, say, 1470 and 1500, the historical attack upon the Church seemed overwhelming. It continued to succeed from that day onwards almost into our own time. It was like a great flood which runs at first most violently, gradually slackens, but is long in losing its momentum. Hardly till our own day have we seen that flood come to still water and then begin to recede. Wherever there was a local custom, an old tradition, a crystallized habit, a legend about the liturgy, a doubtful document put forward in support of Catholic truth, the opponent had full play. A huge mass of demonstrably false accretions lay there open to attack, and the field of action for those who hated the Faith seemed unlimited. Even now, when things have changed the other way round and when it is the Catholic who has history on his side and the anti-Catholic who is getting nervous about it, the inherited fashion of historical attack continues in particular sections. The opponents of the Faith have still the good fortune to discover in remote districts misapprehensions of the past, and the less enlightened of our enemies still approach even the main problems under the naive impression that if only they use historical criticism against religion they are bound to win.

Now, this long use of a successful offensive against the Catholic Church, in which the conquering weapon was the appeal to history, had a certain effect upon the Catholic mind from which that mind still suffers. It threw the Catholic mind upon the defensive where history was concerned. A habit of acting upon the defensive grew up and became almost second nature, in this field of history, to the Catholic apologist.

Out of a thousand examples of how this timidity worked let me take the Donation of Constantine.

It was first affirmed by our enemies that the principle of Papal supremacy in jurisdiction reposed upon that document—which it never had. It was then shown that the document did not belong to the date to which it professed to belong. It was then called a forgery—which it certainly was not—and when its spurious character was definitely proved, for it *was* spurious (that is, not an original state action of Constantine's date as it had been supposed to be) the Papal power was proclaimed to have lost its historic foundation. Its support was said to have been destroyed. It could only defend itself by falsehood, by affirming the Donation to be genuine, or what was morally worse, and in reason still more absurd, pretending to ignore it.

Now, how did Catholic apologists in the main behave themselves under this attack? They fell at once upon the defensive; they retreated from position to position. The first doubts had been cast in the fifteenth century; they did not finally abandon the document until the seventeenth century.

The story of the Donation is the story of a large number of points, some more, some less, important, tacked onto what would seem to have been originally the genuine acts of St. Sylvester, the Pope who was contemporary with Constantine. Legends, some fantastic, some merely inaccurate, grew round the genuine record. It was apparently copied and recopied, its lack of historical value increasing with each manipulation, most of which seem to have taken place in the East. The legends grew into myths and were believed. At last, in the darkest moment of learning, they appeared in the West. But though the Document in the form we have it is a mass of inaccuracies, false history and mere fairy tale (part of it about a Dragon), there is a core of truth, as there is in all such things. It rightly presents the Bishop of Rome as obtaining much added temporal power by the transference of the Imperial Office to Byzantium; it notes the gift of the Lateran palace; it is a witness, though a confused and badly warped witness, to the greatly enhanced local jurisdiction of the Papacy after A.D. 323.

If, on reading the first criticisms of this spurious document, their value had been at once admitted, all would have been well. The temporal power of the Papacy was of far older date than the first use of the Donation. There was no need to cling to its authenticity. But men fall into the trap set by conservative habits. They tried to maintain an impossible credence in the document and were inevitably beaten.

The whole affair is an excellent example of the way in which the early historical attack on the Church captured the initiative and proceeded from advance to advance. There grew up, on our side, in connection with the enemies' historical attack an ingrained habit of the defensive.

Now, an ingrained habit of the defensive is the prime condition of defeat. There is no such thing as a defensive battle or a defensive campaign, save in the sense that one may begin on the defensive, but only with the fixed object of turning to the offensive at the right moment. It was not the learning, still less the logic, of our enemies which gave them such strength in this field; it was the defensive mood into which Catholic apologists allowed themselves to be maneuvered. That defensive mood produced three types of error in tactic.

(a) We were led off on detail and failed to face the historic problem as a whole. We spent energy almost uselessly in answering objections, petty in character or limited in application, which energy we should have better employed in showing the absurdity of the whole anti-

Catholic spirit in history.

(b) As a necessary sequence of getting entangled in detail we let much go by default, which we ought to have maintained; we accepted the enemies' statements on a mass of matters where they were quite wrong and could have been proved wrong.

(c) We allowed our own minds to be warped, if not against Catholicism, at any rate against true history; and we fell (especially where we were citizens of anti-Catholic countries) into accepting for national heroes, or for the heroes of civilization in general, men who were the enemies of the Faith and for their villainous opposites men who were, if not defenders of the Faith, at any rate typical of the Catholic culture.

As an example of being led off into details, let us take three cases, each of which has raised a great deal of controversy in its time: The word DIVUS, or an abbreviation of it, appearing before the name of a saint, especially of a canonized pope in a church or public monument; the misunderstanding of the word INFALLIBILITY; the misunderstanding of the doctrine of INDULGENCES. In all these cases we have been concerned with the ignorance of our opponents; we have given special attention to them because that ignorance was easily exposed and our task was facile; we were certain of its conclusions; we had only to show (and did show in countless replies) that the word DIVUS was equivalent to holy, and did not mean Divine; that INFALLIBILITY is not impeccability; and does not imply anything outside a very limited field; and that INDULGENCES are not a permission to commit sin, nor even a forgiveness of sin. These, and any number of other limited examples of particular ignorance in anti-Catholics, were made a sort of stock in trade by Catholics in their defensive controversy during modern times.

Now, I am not denying that such details must be dealt with; still less that the exposure of our opponents' ignorance on details is a very valuable result to obtain. I think it is. I rejoice whenever the absurd provincial lack of acquaintance with elementary and important Catholic things is exposed; for as there is nothing more irritating than pride, so there is nothing more satisfactory than the humbling thereof; and as of two opposing philosophies the one which is certain and knows why it is certain must triumph over the one which falters, the undermining of our opponents' certitudes, even in details, is well worth while. I might add that controversy upon detail is nearly always an entertaining occupation. It permits appeal to documents and figures—proved facts; it sometimes gives opportunity for retaliation, and is altogether a very amusing pastime, especially if one holds the trumps.

But my contention is that this allowing of ourselves to be pinned to details involves a loss of power and is not the right way to conduct the struggle, especially at the present moment, when the historical argument has turned in our favor, through additions to knowledge—for a little learning leads men away from the Truth; a large learning confirms the Truth.

I might add another point in connection with this entanglement in detail. I have just instanced three obvious cases of ignorance on the part of our opponents, but in too many cases we undertook the defense of detailed positions with insufficient weapons. We allowed the enemy to choose his point of attack, though we ought to have known that he came up with all the instruments at his disposal and with all the ammunition.

If you look around the field of modern attack on Religion you will find perpetually recurring examples of this.

An enemy of the Faith accumulates a vast mass of facts which go to support some truth—more often only a half-truth—which Catholics may not like to hear and are hitherto, most of them, unfamiliar with. He lays his plans, and springs the hitherto unlikely truth (or half-truth) upon us with an expression of innocent intention. We rush up to defend the position and find ourselves out-gunned. We had no idea there were so many facts carefully hidden and prepared for our discomfiture.

A good example of this is the recent allegation that Clement VII proposed bigamy to Henry VIII. The average educated Catholic with no special reading of the period indignantly denies that any Pope could have done anything so monstrous. He knows it is extremely unlikely; he jumps to the conclusion that it is impossible. But it is not impossible at all. There is no limit to the wickedness or folly of a Pope or any other human being; *unlikely* it is, and the instinct of the average educated Catholic in making an indignant denial was quite right. But he will no doubt be taken by surprise when he has the supposed evidence thrust upon him, and finds himself unable to meet it. "All is as I said," said the opponent (and the opponent here is several hundred of our official or mandarin historians). "Here it is in black and white," and he proceeds to recite the report of Henry's envoy, who writes to his master saying that the Pope had proposed bigamy. The real answer, of course, is: first, that Clement VII *might* have done it; the thing is not physically impossible, nor a contradiction of any theological doctrine on the Papacy; but that, as a fact, he did nothing of the kind. He asked a question: "Did the envoy think that a man could be allowed to have two wives at one time?" which is not at all the same thing as saying that he should be allowed.

But there are examples of whole truths which a Catholic deplores, which in face of the evidence he must admit, but which, if he is not sufficiently acquainted with the evidence, he may be led into denying. For instance, the promise of the same Pope in the matter of allowing the sentence of the Legatine Court to be final. One can indeed argue that a new circumstance had arisen which Clement had not in mind when he gave the promise; but that he gave the promise is history, and—though he might plead that the promise was conditional—he did not keep his word in the sense in which it was taken.

I have said that through this entanglement in detail we suffer the further weakness of allowing much to go by default. We are so much occupied with special points that false statement on a number of others escapes our attention and is permitted to pass muster. There is a mass of such running through all attacks in detail.

One of the best examples I know is the affirmation continually made upon the attitude of ecclesiastical authority towards early chemical research. In this the stock example of detail is a quotation from a Bull of John XXIII* at Avignon. We are told that John XXIII issued a Bull in which he forbade chemical research as impious. The late Professor Bury, Professor of History at Cambridge, an ardent anti-Catholic and a very learned man, repeated this after a hundred others had done so. He affirmed it as a matter of fact in his popular and worthless "History of the Freedom of Thought," which I had the pleasure of analyzing some years ago.[4]

The average educated Catholic would probably meet Bury's statement by saying that the times were uncritical and ignorant, that innovation was naturally suspected, that there might well be a connection between alchemy and occult forbidden practices. But all the while, on the authority of such men as Professor Bury, he was admitting the main fact, that a Bull *had* been issued by John XXIII at Avignon, prohibiting chemical experiments. The Catholic let the chief count in this indictment go by default. *But was such a Bull ever issued?* No! Professor Bury, like any number of learned men, was only copying what he had seen in earlier writings, without taking the trouble to look up his authority. Those who do so will find that the Pope's action, so far from being a prohibition against chemical research, is simply an excellent police ordinance governing the finance and markets at Avignon, and forbidding charlatans to take lead and brass from ignorant people under the pretense of turning them into silver and gold.

This evil we suffer from—getting entangled with detail—is most serious when it takes the form of ourselves accepting all manner of anti-Catholic myths—and this warping of history in our own minds, this acceptation of historical falsehood as a mat-

*That is, Pope John XXII. Due to an historical confusion, the tenth-century Pope John XV was for centuries inaccurately listed as Pope John XVI, with a corresponding error in numbering being continued with subsequent popes. Thus the above-mentioned "Pope John XXIII" (d. 1334) was really Pope John XXII. (Subsequently, there was also an anti-pope, or false claimant to the papal office, who was called John XXIII; he died in 1419.)—*Editor*, 1992.

4. *"How Anti-Catholic History is written."*—C.T.S. [Catholic Truth Society].

ter of course, is at its worst in England, because it may be said that here, as in no other place, nearly all history, until a very recent date, was official; and all our official history was violently anti-Catholic.

When no question of doctrine is affected, a myth which is essentially anti-Catholic in origin goes down the more easily. There is no doctrine involved, for instance, in the great Louis XIV myth. On the contrary, as Louis XIV pushed Gallicanism almost to the limits of rebellion, a Catholic might believe ill things of him. But the motive of the defamation is not his Gallicanism. On the contrary, it is his political defense of Catholicism in general throughout Europe.

No doctrine is involved in the myth; a man might be fervent for every Catholic belief and practice, and it would in no way interfere with these for him to believe that Louis XIV was at once despicable and a monster. When Macaulay confirmed the myth in a rhetorical mixture of ignorance and spite, the English Catholic reader, for whom Macaulay is a classic, accepted the verdict. He accepted it all the more easily because the French king was in the latter part of his reign the enemy of this country. When Macaulay tells him that Madame de Maintenon was bigoted and intolerant, he does so either because he suppresses (or as is more probable, because he does not know) the real character of the woman, with her strong remains of Huguenotry and her distaste for devotions to Our Lady. In the same way the average educated Catholic accepts the same historian's absurd description of the battle of the Boyne. The battle of the Boyne was a rear-guard action fought by a hopelessly outnumbered force against a vastly superior one. The invaders had four times as many guns, nearly twice as many men, and four or five times as many *trained men* as the defending force, yet the Jacobite army retired successfully with the loss of less than six percent of its men and only one gun, and through this successful retirement was able to keep up the war for many months. The official myth which we have all accepted and which has sunk into the minds of Catholics, makes of the Boyne a decisive action in which a disgraceful rout was imposed upon a Catholic army by the valor and skill of their enemies. There is nothing to prevent a good Catholic remaining fervent in faith and practice, although he swallow Macaulay's myth—to give it a polite name. An erroneous view of what happened at the battle of the Boyne does not conflict with any Catholic doctrine. Nevertheless, when we accept it we are accepting history which has been falsified with the special purpose of belittling the Catholic cause.

Perhaps the best example of the way we have of allowing official history to warp our minds is the great Elizabethan fable. Thorold Rogers conclusively showed that during the reign of this unfortunate woman the wealth of England was declining, which was only what one would expect during a period of suppressed civil war and of perpetual insecurity owing to a minority government basing its power on terror. It was, further, only to be expected that English wealth should decline when the principal market for English goods, the Netherlands, was turning into a shambles. It is further demonstrable that Elizabeth was thwarted at every turn; that most of the domestic and most of the foreign policy carried out in her name was distasteful to her; that the bulk of her people at the beginning of her reign and still something like half of them even towards the end of it, sympathized—as did the unhappy woman herself—with the old religious traditions of the English, and not with the new Calvinism; that a married clergy was as odious to them as to her. All this we are hardly allowed to hear. The myth is established, repeated, confirmed. A glorious queen, at the head of a nation as enthusiastic as herself for the destruction of Catholicism, proceeds from one triumph to another; lays the foundations of our present Empire overseas and develops commerce upon every side. The piracies of the day are trumpeted as the noble actions of national heroes, etc., etc.

So thoroughly have we been steeped in this nonsense that not many years ago a great Catholic family gave a pageant in the grounds of their country house, the theme of which was the splendor of Elizabeth. I hope her spirit is now at rest and was able to follow the scene, for she was a witty woman, and the absurdity would have delighted her hugely.

Well, if the habit of the defensive involves us in all this weakness, the lesson is that the counter-offensive should now be our policy. We have every reason for undertaking it, in theory and in practice; in theory because to remain permanently upon the defensive is to lose the campaign (and we have been on the defensive now for generations), but in practice also, because the weight of historical argument is now on our side.

The weight of true history was always on our side, because truth confirms truth. What is true in theology—the Queen of Sciences—will be true in the subsidiary departments such as history. But the moment is particularly propitious because recent research, and the conclusions based upon a wider knowledge of documents, particularly support us today; while we have another practical reason for taking action, which is that the moment in which we are living is disillusioned. The belief of people in the historical fairy tales of the last generation, as in all its other old traditions both true and false, is shaken. Our difficulty lies neither in the quality of our weapons nor in our disposal of them, nor with the absence of a sufficient field in which to use them, but rather with getting an audience.

The younger generation today are perfectly willing to hear the truth—for instance, about the period of the Reformation. They are more than willing to revise the old-fashioned and already more than half-forgotten misrepresentations of Catholic times and Catholic nations, and meanwhile the instruments with which to act are there ready to our hands.

But we shall not use them with effect unless we act upon certain directives, unless we are inspired by certain rules; and here, passing from the negative to the positive, I shall, I know, be on ground where dispute arises as vigorously amongst Catholics themselves as between Catholics and their opponents. But I cannot put forward a view which is not my own; I must express what I hold, for my readers to accept or refuse it.

There seem to me to be three main rules which should give us our directives in the counter-attack which is already overdue, and the forward movement for the recovery of true history.

The first is that to which I alluded in the previous paper in connection with a larger subject: a spirit of hostility; or, if the phrase be preferred—a phrase consonant with the metaphors used throughout these pages—a spirit of the offensive; that spirit of the offensive without which a counter-attack fails.

The second directive, derived from this hostile spirit prepared for the attack against our opponents, is a readiness to analyze *false method* in history as well as false fact, and to replace it by a true method.

The third directive is the necessity of working upon the largest lines, and of taking history as a whole. There will always be plenty of secondary points to be dealt with of minutiae and even of petty local action, but the main outline of historical truth must be at once our object and the controlling consideration in all that we do.

I will take these necessary directives, as I see them to be, in their order; and first the one which will be the most easily challenged and which is most repugnant to our modern convention—hostility.

I say that we must approach our historical task in a spirit hostile to our opponents. We must look with suspicion upon every statement; still more upon the main tendencies in writing which we instinctively feel to be opposed to Catholic truth, even where they do not overtly attack that truth. We must not begin by accepting the bulk of official stuff and then see where we can pick holes in it to the advantage of religion. We must rather set out with a general suspicion of the whole cargo. We must consider the official history that has been presented to us as something which has already been put upon its first trial, has been found wanting, and appears in the final court weighted with the presumption of untruth. We must ask, upon all the official heroes presented to our admiration, whether their story is truly told, and expect the answer to be in the negative. We must do the same by the official villains. We must be forever looking narrowly at terms and expressions which may be used to convey a false impression indirectly while avoiding mere errors in dates and reference. We must treat the matter before us, as it has hitherto been presented by the mass of anti-Catholic writers, as we would treat the statement of a man often discovered in falsehood or unpardonable ignorance; we must look equally narrowly for *suppressio veri* [the suppression of truth], that master weapon of the other side.

That is the spirit we must cultivate; that is the spirit in which alone permanent and valuable results on a large scale will be achieved.

I may be told that those whose repeated falsehoods we have to expose, and whose warped presentation of the past it is our business to render ridiculous, act more often than not in good faith; that it is lunacy to imagine a vast conspiracy against the truth on the part of men, very few of whom would be of the caliber to undertake anything of the sort, and a great part of whom are no worse than worthy drones copying each other's work in an endless chain and providing history "made to sell," suitable to the public school and examination system. That is perfectly true; but it is not to the point, any more than it would be to the point in a war to remind one's troops that individuals of the enemy were, in their civilian capacity, worthy husbands and fathers. We have a campaign to win and a decisive result to achieve; it is no business of ours whether Professor This or Mr. That were in good faith when they said (for instance) that the English people drove out James II; or that the Whigs under William III and his sister-in-law saved England; or that the House of Commons was a national and representative body under Elizabeth; or that Henry VIII was ever careful to be in good touch and sympathy with the mass of his subjects; or that the medieval statutes restricting the encroachments of Papal taxation were all one with the Tudor statutes destroying the connection between England and the Universal Church. Many men write these things down from a sort of mental inertia because it is easier to keep in a rut, many more because falsehood is in their traditions and they would feel shocked at the appearance of the truth. Many others because it is all part and parcel of the making of their livelihoods, and because true history in its first beginnings does not sell; only conventional history provides an income. There are even many so ignorant that they actually have not heard how and where their conventional attitude is false, and they have colleagues thoroughly habituated to that curious irrational faculty whereby men divide their minds into various compartments, believing with one compartment what another compartment would inform them to be false. With all that, I say, we are not concerned. We have two weapons and two weapons only, but they are invincible—that we possess the truth and that we use our reason. Our advantage against our opponents is that they are supporting falsehood in whatever degree of consciousness they may be, and that, having a false theology, they do not reason clearly nor distinguish between the probable and improbable in human motive. We must use those weapons unsparingly, without troubling ourselves over the good or bad faith of those against whom we use them. The struggle is arduous, and unless we use our full strength we shall not succeed.

The second directive I have postulated, deriving from this proper spirit of hostility towards our opponents, is a lively activity in analyzing their false historical method and replacing it by right historical method.

For instance, they work upon a false psychology; we must meet it by a true psychology. When they tell us that, deplorable as was the loot of the Church in the sixteenth century, it was but an adjunct to the religious zeal of the reformers, which was the true driving power, we must point out that that is a contradiction of what is known as human motive. Not one man in five hundred is more strongly moved by an ideal than by the prospect of immediate gain. There is no compromise, no wriggling of the conscience, no plumb baseness to which men will not descend for the getting of great wealth suddenly.

A vast economic revolution such as that which despoiled religion throughout the Protestant culture, and especially in England, for the benefit of individual princes, nobles, squires, merchants and adventurers, and was continued (especially in this country) by the savage dispossession of Catholic laymen and the transference of their wealth to their enemies, is the dominating fact of the Reformation. Those who worked the movement to their enrichment took advantage of genuine religious excitement in a few brave, sincere, and often unbalanced, men; but it was not these last who made England Protestant—it was a pack of robbers.

Again, in this matter of method we must insist particularly upon the value of tradition as against the document. It is not in dealing with the comparatively recent history of the Reformation, but rather with the origins of the Catholic Church and with her earliest records in the New Testament and sub-apostolic writings, that this false method most needs to be exposed. Upon a word or two in a document, a phrase of the vaguest kind, those who would destroy the Faith pile up a monstrous scaffolding of guesswork and unsupported assertion, while to the great stream of tradition they pay no heed at all. What method could be more false?

There is also in the historical work directed against the Catholic Church one particular false method so puerile that one is almost ashamed to expose it, and yet it is universally present; it is the method of taking documentary points out of proportion to the whole body of known facts and building upon them some unwarrantable conclusion. By leaving out all the mass of converging evidence upon the other side this method can achieve any result at will. Think what a formidable body of evidence, for instance, the future historian, armed with sufficient machinery for research, could build up to show that the England of Queen Victoria was strongly Prohibitionist. Tradition, common sense, a host of allusions to daily habits, ten thousand pictures, and perhaps the relics of as many public-houses would be there to tell an opposite story; but by the simple process of quoting only those points which support your thesis you could make a plausible case, in the ears of the ignorant at least, for even so monstrous a case as that. I say that this piece of false method is puerile in its simplicity, but those of us who are accustomed to dealing with anti-Catholic history in controversy can testify that it is ubiquitous, for that is exactly the way they go on about the origins of the sacramental system, of the hierarchy, of the Papacy.

Or, again, take this example of false method: confining the national story to the boundaries of the nation alone, so omitting that general background of foreign affairs in the light of which alone can domestic affairs become comprehensible. What value has the story of Mary Stuart, for instance, unless the rivalry of France and Spain be made the *main* factor therein? Or who can understand the Protestant and plutocratic destruction of the English Yeoman in the seventeenth and eighteenth centuries unless he sees, contemporary and in contrast with that destruction, the upbuilding of a fine peasantry in Catholic Europe?

But the worst of all false methods, by which more than by any other is anti-Catholic history propagated today, the one which appeals most of all to the ignorant general reader and the one which it is most difficult to eliminate wholly even from the mind of the best instructed, is the method of reading modern times into the past.

Anti-Catholic history swarms with this kind of thing, especially today and especially here in England. Take, for instance, one most glaring example, the burning of heretics under Mary. This bout of vigorous repression had certain abnormal characteristics about it; it was thrust upon the religious courts by the Council and the lay power. It crowded into a short time more executions for heresy than had been seen in a century or more. It was undertaken on religious grounds, where it should more properly have fallen under the civil criminal law, whereby its revolutionary victims would have been condemned for treason rather than for false doctrine. But what was most emphatically *not* abnormal in it was the form of the execution—burning. To us in our time and place, burning is abnormal; so horrible that we dare not use our imaginations upon it. Everywhere in the white world (except in the more Protestant parts of the United States of America) it has disappeared, and even there it is no longer legal, but an illegal action, though a tolerated one. But a man who represents burning in the 1550's as abnormal is as grossly unhistorical as would be a future writer who should represent flogging in prisons today [1931] as abnormal, or long inquisitorial secret examination of suspects by the police as abnormal. These proceedings also may rouse such indignation in some future age (which will doubtless have much worse things of its own) as to stamp our age with atrocious cruelty, moral and physical. But that does not make it sound history to say that in our age they are universally execrated. For we all know that they are not. So with burning in the past. It was not peculiar to prosecutions for heresy. Witches were burnt in ardently Calvinist Scotland for nearly two lifetimes after the Marian persecutions. There was no general protest against the practice, and they were burnt in very much larger numbers than ever heretics had been. Men were burnt for unnatural vice and women were burnt upon the plea of decency to save their being hanged. Wives convicted of poisoning their husbands were burnt much more than a hundred years after Mary's death. That rather priggish diarist, Evelyn, notes with a passing pity, but without any indignation, seeing a woman being burnt alive in Smithfield as he took his walks abroad; he notes it and then proceeds to talk of other things which interest him more. The last woman to be burnt in London suffered in front of the Old Bailey, in May 1789, long after the American War of Independence, and almost on the eve of the French Revolution.

To take another example, the conception of the House of Commons as the natural organ of government and as the representative body of the English people. To talk of action done without its leave under Charles I as "unconstitutional"; to call this body under Burghley, summoned by an all-powerful executive and often individually chosen by the Crown "The nation"; to call its pronouncements "the opinion of the country"—all that stuff is grossly unhistorical. It is reading the present, or rather the nineteenth century, into the sixteenth century and the seventeenth century. Yet by this method a good half of the apologetics for the destruction of Catholicism in England is inspired. You read of the Elizabethan House of Commons passing Cecilian resolutions for the killing of Mary Stuart and you are left, and intended to be left, under the impression that the voice was that of the English people in unison.

And the third directive (which seems to me the most important) is the dealing with our historical apologetic and the restoration of historical truth upon the *largest* lines.

Hitherto the Catholic argument has perpetually turned, as I have said, upon minor points, details of particular controversy in biography or clerical history. We have been concerned to explode particular legends, to defend individuals against particular slanders, to rehabilitate defamed characters, and conversely to attack false minor statements made upon matters where such statements could be used for the ridicule or weakening of the Catholic position. Such particular work has its place, though very often we must admit it has led us into positions from which we have had to retreat; but no accumulation of it can supply the effect of work upon general lines.

For example, we should emphasize the moral health and joy which accompanied the Catholic culture, and contrast the unhealthy gloom of the spirit originating with Calvin. *That* is at once an historical truth and an historical argument of the highest value. Or, again, we have the general truth that the catastrophe whereby the religious unity of Europe made shipwreck four hundred years ago was an accident and a blunder which might have been avoided, and would have been avoided by greater sincerity on the reforming side, on the other by a larger measure of humility and intelligence, and by less sloth, avarice and worldliness. Or, again, we can show vigorously how the transformation of the Roman world and its conversion to Catholicism saved what could be saved of the general Pagan culture and made the resurrection of Europe possible. Or, again, we can emphasize the soundly historical nature of Catholic origins, the remote roots of the Papacy, of the Mass, of all that is characteristically Catholic today. Or, again, we can engage on the vigorous and bold demonstration of miracle, the continued affirmation of our historical proof of miracle; not a timid, half-hearted excuse for possible miracle, but a hearty, intellectual contempt for those who say *a priori* that miracle is impossible and a hammering well in of the truth that miracles *have* happened and that the historical proofs for them are conclusive.

All this lies to our hand and should be the major directive of the counter-offensive.

The Catholic Church is more than the sum of its parts. It is an organic and vital thing, like a nation. It has a life as vigorous as ever after twenty centuries. It is the thing which saved the world and in the weakening of which our general civilization may perish. To put *that* picture in a lively way before the mind of our generation is the chief task before us.

A LETTER TO AN ANGLO-CATHOLIC FRIEND

The people strangely calling themselves "Anglo-Catholic" [i.e., Anglicans] are the nearest to us in mood, just as the skeptic is the nearest to us in intelligence. Yet their intellectual position is as Protestant as any, for they do not admit unity as the test of the Visible Church. There is a Person and a Voice. It has authority. The Anglo-Catholic does not follow that authority, and as for the Voice and the Features, he has them only by reflection or portraiture. He is not in their presence. Let him come there.

7

A LETTER TO AN ANGLO-CATHOLIC FRIEND

We of the Faith have heard for now many years past the thesis which you present. It affects us in a special manner.

It is but one of very many which reach our ears. We are, in Protestant countries, daily insulted. We are also reproached courteously, jostled with indifference, attacked crudely from all manner of positions, by those who can make nothing of us and who, from the very little they know of true religion, are moved by it to contempt and hostility. For the Faith seems to them an absurdity in this world of the senses, where knowledge upon the ultimate things is hidden from the direct gaze of men.

But the one thesis which you present has for us a special interest of its own, because it is sympathetic.

I have confessed for myself (it is a purely personal confession) that I am more in sympathy with the skeptic than with any of the enemies opposed to that which is the sole solution of our riddles and therefore the salvation of mankind: the only House. It is my fault, perhaps; and certainly my misfortune. The skeptic thinks more than he feels, and there I am with him—or rather, I take thinking to come before feeling: wherein I have a quarrel with the Seraphim. But no matter.

Among all those outside the famous boat of the Fisherman you are most in sympathy with us.

The skeptic does not sympathize with us at all. We sympathize with him—which is a poor substitute. We say to ourselves: "At least this man uses his reason, on such postulates as are common to the human race." This moves our hearts towards him, especially in such a time as ours when men have ceased to reason. But he does not correspondingly say that *we* reason. As a rule he knows nothing about us, and too often he is, in these days of mechanics, deplorably uncultured.

But you who call yourselves Anglo-Catholics have the heart, if not the root, of the matter in you. That living force which has transformed the world makes for unity, and you know it. Moreover, you know its name, which is the Incarnation. Its manifestations are not only familiar to you, but loved by you. You would accept: in a fashion you *have* accepted. You desire to undo (only in your own province, oddly enough, and not, as reason should demand, throughout the world) the almost-murder of Christendom in the sixteenth and seventeenth centuries. You desire unity, not mechanically, but organically. You are athirst for the Living Truth: you proclaim it, and in a fashion you follow it.

Now to you thus situated we appear wrongly. You misunderstand the Church. You take our outline for our substance, our manifestations for our essentials, and our manner for our being.

I will attempt in this very short space to put before you the problem as it appears to us.

The essential in our judgment (we of the Faith) is that there stands on earth an Individual to be recognized as we recognize human individuals—by the voice, the gesture, the expression.

The chain of reason is complete. Is there a God? Yes. Is He personal? Yes. Has He revealed Himself to men? Yes. Has He done so through a corporation—a thing not a theory? Has He created an organism by which He may continue to be known to mankind for the fulfillment of the great drama of the Incarnation? Yes.

Where shall that organism be found? There is only one body on earth which makes such a claim: it is the Catholic Roman Apostolic Church. That claim we of the Faith accept. The consequences of that acceptation are innumerable, satisfactory and complete. We are at home. No one else of the human race is at home.

Now to this you answer that such an organism (the Visible

Church), being worked by men and through men and being (because it is visible) of this world (as well as of the other world for which and by which it is), suffers the faults of humanity. On that all are agreed. Only fools confuse the vices of officials, their occasional and abominable corruptions, with the essential of what they serve: and you are not a fool. But you specially insist upon one part of this truth—that, among other human errors is abuse of authority, the exaggeration of a claim by those whose claim is justified. You maintain that there may be periods of doubt and chaos, that we have been passing through one such period (has it not lasted a long time?) and that, during the misunderstanding, the Visible Church, though it still exists, is in suspension, and that meanwhile you are part of it.

Why, then, let me invite you to definition. It is not an idle nor a mechanical invitation. It is not a matter of logomachy. Can we not recognize this Visible Church? Can we not know it for what it is? Does not personality involve recognition? Can any person be himself, if none can recognize him, if he do not bear marks of his individual character by which he may be known?

The Visible Church cannot have nationality for its mark: nationality is in a different category; it is wholly human; it is mortal, however deeply loved. How can the Universal Authority be national? How can it continue indefinitely without a form? *Ubi est Christus?* [*Where is Christ?*] If you answer as I would, and as would any man of our sort, "He is in those who follow Him in the spirit and in truth," I agree—though I am not much given to words of that kind. Holiness is everywhere*. You may find it in pagans at one end of the scale, as in foolish emotionalists at the other, though I confess I find it with increasing frequency in those who are of the Faith, and fully in communion. But where is the holy Institution?

---

*The author is obviously using the term "holiness" in a loose sense. The more accurate term would have been "goodness." Goodness can exist on the natural plane and does not necessarily entail the possession of Catholic faith and Sanctifying Grace, as does holiness. —*Editor*, 1992.

You are debarred both by your intelligence and by your particular profession of belief from defining the Church as the collection of all those who show some virtue, or as the vague cohort of those who more or less follow a divine model. You will not advance the plea that individual holiness is enough and a Church unessential. You are not (to use the tiresome modern term) "subjectivists." You know well enough, if others do not, that a Church is necessary, that there is somewhere a Church and this Church is not a theory, but a thing. You know that a thing is or is not, and that reality is apprehended by the human mind, not created by it. Further, you know that a thing only *is* because it is *one*. Now what say you on the mark of unity?

You know very well, indeed it is the very core of your character and teaching, that the Church is the lighthouse of mankind across the night sea-journey of this world. Well, then, in the place of *"Ubi est Christus,"* put this plain question: *"Ubi est Ecclesia? [Where is the Church?]*" Have you seen the majestic face? Have you heard the authoritative voice? The face may be warped through media of perception, the voice may be confused by instruments of transmission. But have you so much as seen that face unmistakable, or heard that voice in its indubitable tone? Can you affirm Personality of that ill-defined abstraction which you propose as an Authority?

Can you speak of divided Christendom in the tone of one who meets a lost friend at last and cries, "I know you. These are the features. This is the Voice"?

If you cannot, then you have not found the Church. Love of nation will not find the Church, nor will habit, still less the following of ease.

There is a city full, as are all cities, of halt and maimed, blind and evil and the rest; but it is the City of God. There are not two such Cities on earth. There is One.

On Legend

There is Legend and there is Myth. Legend is a story told for beauty and edification; it does not pretend to be a true story, it only says that its morals are true. But all Legends, or very nearly all, have in them a valuable core of historical truth. A man is a thoroughly bad historian who despises legend and will not accept it as one of the sources of history. Myth is a false story which is put forward as true. Being a lie, it does harm always and should be eradicated. To create and accept myths is a universal failing of the human mind. Of this evil, as of all evils, the Faith is the best solvent. There was never a time or place when more numerous or more monstrous myths were swallowed whole than the time and place in which we live; and that is because they have not the Faith.

8

ON LEGEND

To understand what Legend is, its value and its sanctity, in many cases its *nutritive* value, is a strong need of our time. For our time is one in which Legend has been so much neglected as almost to fall out of use. Yet upon Legend our fathers were very properly fed, and Legend has filled all Europe with the loveliest, most permanent and most useful writings. In the place of Legend we have today what I will call *Myth,* that is, falsehood passing for historical truth: and how Myth contrasts with Legend, I will ask later on.

A Legend may be thus defined: It is a story told about some real person, real virtue, or real spiritual experience, and of such a quality that it illuminates and satisfies the recipient while it amplifies and gives further substance to the matter to which it is attached.

Thus a Legend may be wholly true although it contains marvelous episodes and is cast into artistic form, or it may be, and usually is, full of detail which no one pretends to be true, a mere piece of fiction; but a piece of fiction—and that is the important point!—relating to, exalting, and fixing in the mind, reality of permanent value. It is in the essence of Legend that its historical value is not in question. It has not to be believed as witness to event but as example; or even as no more than a picture which does us good by its beauty alone. We are not, in using legend, affirming a belief in a particular occurrence, but listening with profit to a story; and if the moral of the story is sound—if its effect is towards truth, goodness, beauty—that is all we ask of it. Humanity has always lived on such stories, and when a false philosophy banishes them or lets them die out, humanity is starved.

The reason why Legend fell out of fashion, was abused and ridiculed and at last almost lost, was that men fell into a habit of measuring everything exactly and neglecting whatever could not be exactly measured. That has been the great intellectual disease of our time, and it arose from the success achieved in physical and other sciences through exact measurement.

Obviously a piece of fiction, or even a piece of picturesque truth handed down by those who were not troubling about evidence, but only about moral truth and beauty, was not acceptable to men who had fallen into this mechanical mood. They asked, when they heard of St. George and the Dragon, where the combat took place and whether the picture of the Dragon was that of a real and known beast. When they heard it was but a tale with a moral to it, they had no use for it. In the same way, an inhuman child on being told, to make him courageous and chivalrous, the story of Jack the Giant Killer, might ask to be shown the site of the Giant's Castle on the ordnance map. On learning that there never was such a castle, the little prig would conclude, I suppose, that facing odds was silly.

Further, men's minds can sink to a level of muddlement in which they confuse the nature of a tale. The fact that so much in Legend was not historically true, led them to call Legend of its nature a lying thing. But the neglect of Legend has led to much greater falsehoods than the use of Legend ever did.

Legend has taken a terrible revenge. For in its absence men have been condemned to Myth, which is the dogmatic affirmation of something false.

The generation which no longer listened to the story of the miraculous bird at whose singing one hundred years passed like one hour, came to deny immortality and eternal beatitude. That is what happens when men are starved of Legend. Therefore, we should all pray that Legend may return.

It is perfectly true, of course, that Legend always may, and sometimes does, turn into Myth, and society must be on its guard against that. You have here a parallel in the degradation of images to false uses. That noble and admirable part of true religion which appears in our devotion to holy images may, by exaggeration, lapse into idolatry. But as between a contempt for holy images and some excess of devotion to them, we know very well on which side the worst evils of society are prone to arise.

It is an error to exaggerate devotion to a shrine, as did that French King who secretly stole money from Our Lady of Paris to give it to Our Lady of Tours. But to pay no attention to shrines has far worse results. So it is with legend.

When a Legend becomes a Myth, that is, when what is undoubtedly not historically true is affirmed to be historical truth and used as such in policy and practice, then you have something evil. But you have a much more poisonous evil when the mind has come to despise instinctively almost any story that is beautifully and spiritually true and illuminating, merely because it may not be historical.

Legend ranges from the fairy story at one end of the spectrum to the exquisitely told and admirably illustrated true anecdote at the other end; while in between lies the great mass of legends which have in them a greater or less proportion of historical fact, but nearly always the same proportion of value to holiness and right living.

Take for instance two stories, one of the first kind, historically true, the other not. The first is in a book about St. Louis, written by a contemporary who knew the King well. It is a plain historical fact of which he was an eye witness, and which yet might well have grown to be ridiculed as a legend if the text of the book had been lost.

It is the story of how the holy King, sitting in the cabin with his family on his way to the Crusades, felt the ship suddenly heeling over and in peril; how he went up on deck and asked the captain what gust that was; and how the captain answered: "It was not one of the four great Winds of Heaven, but only a foolish little wind which we call in these parts the little Guerbin wind," whereupon St. Louis marveled and said to those about him: "See how great is God, Who, when He proposes to put in peril the King of France himself and all his royal blood, uses not one of His four major winds, but a wretched little wind called the Guerbin wind of which no one has ever heard!"

Now that might perfectly well have been turned into a Legend with a very slight alteration. The Legend might have been that the King of France was holding forth on the greatness of God; how in the midst of his discourse this accident happened; how it seemed to him miraculously apposite, and how he used it to point the moral. Such a legend would have made a slightly more rounded story, but it would have been substantially true as mere history, and utterly true in morals and theology; yet those who despise legend would have left the historic truth forgotten and the moral truth unemphasized.

The other example is a legend which has probably no historical element in it at all, but which I shall particularly cherish so long as I have breath, for I find it the most pleasing and sustaining of legends: I mean the Legend of St. Christopher, who, carrying on his shoulders a little child across a river, felt the weight growing till it nearly bore him down; for the little child was the Redeemer of the World.

We know hardly anything of St. Christopher. I would rather have said, "We know nothing," were I not afraid of some learned champion coming out with a contradiction. At any rate, we know precious little, and I shouldn't wonder if he never lived.

Nevertheless, his big good-natured giant image was in the entry of churches all up and down Europe. Rationalism got rid of it. It has come back in the most unexpected way through motor cars. I am not sure that they are wise, by the way, to make it a mascot for motor cars. I have my suspicions that that great Ferryman, in his simplicity, thinks, as often as not, that he is being asked to ferry people over the last river of all, to the shores of which motor cars have a justified reputation for driving us.

Be that as it may, the Legend is invaluable. It is the Legend of service as one road to beatitude. As the poet says:

"You bore the weight of all the wears of the world
When that you bore my weakness, Christopher."

Now in contrast with this main use of Legend as an example and illuminant (of which the Legend of St. Christopher is an excellent example) let us consider another use it has—the retention, incorporated with lovely story, of fact that would otherwise be lost—the use of Legend as a witness to history.

In this sort I know of none more misunderstood or more valuable than the Legend of Glastonbury; and as it *may* be almost wholly unhistorical and is still generally thought to be so, it is of special value as an illustration.

I pass by Glastonbury once a year at least; and often more than once in the same year. Every time I see that famous hill I marvel at the way in which England is now cut off from her living past.

Glastonbury ought to be one of the half dozen most famous places in Europe. It was one of the half dozen most famous places for certainly a thousand years and probably for thirteen or fourteen hundred years. It is now a place in which certain tourists, not many of them, come and gape at ruins; but it means nothing more to England at large. A handful of the educated classes know what it means, but England as a whole no longer remembers.

What should we say if Italy dealt thus with the steep hill of Cassino, or France with the rock of St. Michael, or the Spaniards with Santiago? What should we say if Rheims meant no more to the French than Glastonbury does to the English?

Yet Glastonbury meant much more than any of these. It meant much more even than Santiago. It was the premier shrine of all the west. It counted as an apostolic thing founded within a few years of the Crucifixion.

Of course the story is legendary, but most Legends have history behind them and, take it by and large, there is more history in Legend by far than fantasy. Especially is this true of legends of very high antiquity.

The legend is this. St. Joseph of Arimathea, that rich man who was wise enough to pay for the entombment of Our Lord, came here with companions bringing with him relics of the Last Supper, especially the chalice; and he here founded a shrine which has since endured.

I am sure I appear absurd when I say that I believe this legend to contain historical truth. There grew up accretions which are probably no more than beautiful stories and not historically true. Some of these marvelous or unlikely things may well be true; for it is always a safe rule in history to lean strongly on the side of tradition, but at any rate one may or must admit that in most legend there is this element of fantasy.

But I see nothing impossible or even improbable in these stories of wanderings during the Apostolic age. People who sneer at the stories and think they are showing an "historical mind" are doing the very reverse. They are unable to put themselves in the shoes of the men of a long-past time.

It is certain that the effect produced by Our Lord's ministry and Passion and Resurrection upon the comparatively small circle which received the original impression of those tremendous things was very strong indeed. The proof that it was so is that the Church is to be found, within living memory of those events, spread throughout civilization. It is certain that the men who received those impressions were burning to convey them to others at the expense of long journeys and of great perils. Why should they not have reached the limits of the west?

The topography of Glastonbury exactly suits the story.

It was a port in a lagoon in those days—a shallow sea, now replaced by a flat, marshy plain. One can see to this day how the old Roman road approached, not directly as it would have done if Glastonbury had been surrounded by dry land, but by a ferry over the narrow piece of intervening water. It is exactly like the approach of the Roman road to what was then the Island of Thanet.

The little church of wattles which was the first one to be built at Glastonbury was carefully preserved and was set within a new building to keep it intact during later centuries. There is good evidence for that. It was a British shrine in the Roman times. The evidence that Arthur was buried here is perfectly good traditional evidence, only rejected by people who do not know what traditional evidence is.

It must have been, therefore, already a place of reverend antiquity at the end of the Roman Empire, and that it should have had an Apostolic origin would be no more fantastic than the fact that St. Thomas preached in the Indies. You have not contemporary documents, but you have a most powerful rooted tradition. And people who think that traditions of that kind arise out of nothing are incapable of understanding mankind or its story.

Whether the chalice of the Last Supper really was brought there or not no one can say, because here tradition is confused by the mass of contradictory later stories. That the Chalice should have been preserved is common sense. One may legitimately doubt relics of any great personality if they date from a period before he had affected his generation, but it is foolish to deny relics coming from a period *after* he had affected it powerfully.

One may doubt a relic of the Holy Infancy; but why doubt relics of the Passion?

I take it that the relics of the Passion were preserved. It seems to me normal that they should have been. The burden of proof against the Table of the Last Supper being at Rome, for instance, or against the Nails, or the Fragments of the Crown of Thorns, or the Lance of Longinus which the Crusaders found in Antioch, is not upon those who rely upon tradition, but upon their opponents.

However, the legend of the Chalice having been buried at Glastonbury (or rather on the hill opposite, called Wearyall) is not on the same basis as the rest. But the rest is reasonable. The name of St. Joseph was associated with Glastonbury as far back as the story can be traced. The place was obviously held from the furthest antiquity in the highest reverence. Right up to the great pre-Reformation councils Glastonbury had precedence over all other monastic establishments in the West. The Apostolic origin of Glastonbury was unquestioned. Glastonbury may well date from the first century.

A hundred years ago to say that would have seemed mad; thirty years ago it would still have seemed perverse; today it seems absurd; tomorrow it will be evenly debated and probably, in another lifetime, admitted. That is the way with truths that are based on tradition. They come into their own in time.

But it is true that Legend is always liable to create Myth, and Myth is an evil.

The word "Myth" can be, and is, used in all sorts of ways. It is used to mean a merely symbolic story, such as that of Mithras or the masonic business of Hiram which no one was ever expected to take for history; and it is used (inaccurately) as equivalent to Legend.

I am here using it in a definite and limited sense: "False history passing as true."

It is an evil, and a particularly noxious one, for it gives false leadership.

The observation of the world over, say, forty active years, from early manhood to the approach of sixty, gives one a fine panorama of Myth; how a Myth arises, how it is formed, hardens, becomes accepted, and passes at last into a sort of public dogma. There is the Myth about People, the Myth of Theory, and the Myth of Event. And all three are discovered by experience to follow the same lines of development. After a certain number of years one has the plan of it in one's mind, as one might have the plan of development in a vegetable from seed to fruit.

* * *

First of all comes a statement about a Person, or an Event, or a Theory; about, for instance, the innocence or guilt of an accused Person, say, Dreyfus or the Tichborne claimant, or about the reality or falsehood of a particular Event, such as the phrase attributed to Galileo: "and yet it moves"; or about its character, such as the real causes of the outbreak of a war; or a statement that such and such a Theory truly solves a particular problem; as, for instance, the theory that a glorious (but imaginary) "Nordic Race" composed of people oddly like ourselves solves the problem "How do things get done?"

For a longer or shorter period, usually a shorter one, the statement appeals to a small body of people. They are fervent, and they propagate it with all their power. Although the statement is false, they believe it to be true. It is hardly in human nature for the deliberate falsehood to be propagated with combined cunning and audacity by a great number of people in conspiracy, or for the evidence against it to be suppressed in the same manner. For the diabolical is rare, as holiness is.

The false statement, then, is believed by its affirmers, and the second stage begins with the attack upon it when it becomes more widely known. It shocks the common sense or the experience of average people, and is actively combated. Usually the nascent Myth is killed in infancy by this process. It never takes root; and if it survives at all, it only survives in the despised fanaticism of a few.

But if there enter into the controversy side issues which have logically nothing to do with it, if the controversy arouses passions on matters which the reason should see to be quite distinct from the original statement, *then* at once the breeding soil for Myth, the atmosphere favorable for its growth, has appeared. So that the next stage is the prodigious advance in strength and wide dispersion of the false statement; it is, so to speak, mobilized and armed, and goes out to battle on a large scale.

Even at this stage it may be killed by defeat as like as not.

That is what happened, for instance, to the Myth of the Diamond Necklace just before the Revolution. It was stated by the opponents of Marie Antoinette that she was guilty of theft and falsehood, and that those ultimately condemned were innocent scapegoats, the victims of her malice. Two parties were formed; all the vast revolutionary tide and its enthusiasts favored the Myth; the battle hung even for a matter of seventy years or more, but at the end of a hundred the Myth had been destroyed, and the Truth had taken its place in history. It was quite certain by the last third of the nineteenth century that the Queen was innocent, and all serious historians accept that fact.

But fairly often, the opposite happens. The enthusiasm supporting the Untruth is too strong for its opponents. It conquers; the opposition dwindles; and at last those few who remain firm in their attachment to the Truth remain unheard, or, when they are heard, are treated as cranks. The Myth is then arrived at its maturity, and may so endure, firmly established, for centuries.

Very often what turns the tide in favor of the falsehood is the decay of those interests or of that philosophy which was fighting for the truth, and the universal acceptation of that philosophy which was opposing it. For instance, Patriotism will create a Myth, which the international temper would destroy. In the increase of Patriotism the Myth becomes universal; and it may be noted that the length of human life has a good deal to do with this. When the first generation of combatants dies out, it is usually only one of the two opposing sides which retains enough conviction or interest in the matter to maintain its position.

At long last the Myth is exploded; sometimes not till many hundred years have passed. And when it is exploded a very interesting discovery appears. Amidst the wreck of the Myth are to be found surviving unexpected fragments of Truth.

I have described how the Donation of Constantine is a very good instance of this. It was accepted from about a thousand years ago to about four hundred years ago, and was still vigorously defended until three hundred years ago. Then historical learning destroyed it. For another two hundred years it was treated as merely ridiculous; at last, in our own time, patient research has shown that though it is a Myth and false, it was founded on very valuable Truths.

* * *

I say I have myself had the time to observe the growth of quite a number of Myths, and I admit that the process saddens me. It is not a happy thing to see the firm establishment of untruths, most of which are directly connected with the modern attacks upon Religion. But there is a certain consolation in the comedy of the affair.

One can maintain a permanent grim smile at the extravagance of those faithful to the Myth. Their antics remain amusing.

If a Myth were started that, in the 'eighties of the last century, there had been a unicorn at the Zoo, and if all my children's contemporaries believed it, it would sadden me to see so monstrous though innocuous a lie lording it over the modern mind.

But I confess I should get a good deal of fun out of the hints they would drop. I should hear that because I denied the unicorn, I was a little odd. I was no longer young and had lost my memory. I belonged in youth to a rank of society too humble even to go to the Zoo. I was plainly lying through some religious bias. All that would amuse me.

I have seen one very monstrous Myth reach maturity in my own lifetime, and before my own eyes explode. That was the Myth of Natural Selection. The enthusiasm which supported it and gave it the atmosphere in which to grow was no-Goddism. Natural Selection was believed to have got rid of the necessity for a Creator. Though many who accepted it were innocent of such a motive, *that* was the driving power. Well, it has burst. And a great relief it is to be rid of its presence. It is no longer received. Patriotism and a dislike to confessing error leaves it, especially in this country, some belated supporters; but general opinion has found it out.

Let us hope—against hope—for a similar fate to attend other Myths; especially the worst Myths of official anti-Catholic history. And while the solvent of Myth is evidence reiterated and insisted on, the great palliative is Legend. Let us hammer to ruins the Myth of Elizabethan pirates as conquering heroes, but let us piously cherish that fine Legend, Tennyson's verses on the "Revenge." It will console us for the less pleasant Truth about that nasty fellow Richard Grenville.

The Faith Through The Press

In England at least, a daily Catholic paper is not yet a practical proposition, meaning by this a daily paper not devoted to specifically Catholic news but to all news treated in the light of Catholic philosophy and Catholic morals. What we could and should have is a good general weekly review, but we must face the fact that it would need endowment and without endowment could not flourish or be of effect.

9

THE FAITH THROUGH THE PRESS

I write of a Catholic Press in England; of conditions in the English-speaking countries outside Europe I do not know enough to speak, but I may remark that an English organ of general effect would have its value for the Catholics of all the English-speaking world. There is a Catholic Press all over the place in Ireland, and a solid Catholic Press—by which I mean a Press including daily papers and secular papers of all kinds with a Catholic tone—in every other western country except Great Britain. Holland and Prussia have one, as well as Spain, Italy, France, Bavaria, Austria and Poland. England is the exception even among anti-Catholic nations.

The conditions of a Catholic Press in Great Britain are peculiar to that one society, the people of this island; and I ask myself what manner of Catholic Press could be established here with the full effect which such a Press should be designed for.

There is a large and flourishing Catholic Press already in existence; it is made up of weekly papers and of reviews; it has no daily paper; but to produce the full effect of which I speak the Catholic Press as it now exists, flourishing though it be, needs supplementing. At present it has in all its examples a more or less limited character; highly limited in particular journals which deal only with ecclesiastical subjects, less limited in others, which give their readers general essays and reviews; but, in the case of all it is limited in this sense, that they deal specifically with the Catholic body in this country and mainly with subjects directly attaching to that body as a religious organization.

It may be stated at once that a Press of this character is of very great service and has grown up naturally through the conditions under which Catholics live here. In all countries where the Catholic body is to be found, even where Catholicism is the active religion of the great bulk of the people, there is a Press of this kind, working within the same limits. Such a journal as *La Croix,* in France, is an example, and there are a host of others. But in these countries there is also a more general Press with a Catholic spirit about it; and I maintain that the Catholic Press in Great Britain as it now exists needs something of this kind to supplement it.

We need a Press which shall have a general interest; one in which the effect of Catholicism shall be felt without direct intention, as it were, just as in all the Press around us the effect of anti-Catholicism is manifest, although the editors and readers of that Press would be astonished to hear that this was so. We need a Press in which you may read on any subject of the day—the present controversy on Protection for instance, or the state of affairs in Russia, or a judgment upon fiction, or history, or the stage, which shall give to the reader the opposite implication to anti-Catholicism which he will find in nearly all non-Catholic papers. Until we have such a Press we suffer serious disabilities.

In the first place our way of looking at things (that is, the true way), the sanity for which we stand and the solidity of tradition which it is ours to maintain in a dissolving world, will not, until we have some such general organ, affect anyone outside our own very restricted body. And in the second place, our own people will, until we have such an organ, only be able to get their general reading under anti-Catholic direction. Our people will, in any case, get most of their reading under anti-Catholic direction, for we are citizens of an anti-Catholic society; but had we such a Press as I am here speaking of, the anti-Catholic effect would be corrected. For instance, in a Catholic Press of this kind European affairs would be seen in their proportion; the reader of it could see international problems as they are and not as the anti-Catholic Press presents them through colored spectacles. There would be room for plenty of difference on policy and appreciation of other nations, but, at any rate, the reader of such a Press would occasionally hear that there was something to be said for Poland; that the Germans are not identical with the Prussians of Berlin; that there is a Spanish culture of the very highest value to Europe; that it is in very grave peril through an active anti-national and detestable clique which has seized power; and he would learn something of the great religious quarrel in France, which is of the highest political importance to our time. He would understand how that religious quarrel in France weakened the French at their entry into the war; especially how it weakened them in their failure to negotiate a lasting peace and in their subsequent foreign policy. Much more than this, such a Press would keep general interests in their due proportion; it would not emphasize the horrible or the obscene; it would not prefer tranquillity to justice in the discussion of social affairs.

On sexual matters it would present the old tradition of decency and sound morals; it would present the right apology for property; it would show what authority was and distinguish it from mere force.

Both the effects which it would have, the effect on people outside our body and the effect on people inside it, would be good; the one for the country as a whole, the other for our particular community. It would meet a great need, and I propose to ask myself how that need can be met.

In the first place we must eliminate a false issue; the need is not met by the presence in the Catholic Press as it now exists of articles of general interest. The difference between what is needed and what exists is a difference in proportion. What is needed, not to compete with, still less to diminish, the existing Catholic Press, with its specialization upon particularly Catholic affairs (mainly upon ecclesiastical affairs) is a Press in which *the great bulk* of the printed matter shall be general and even in which ecclesiastical and particularly Catholic affairs shall be absent, save as part of the general news.

You may have an article in *The New Statesman,* for instance, dealing with and ridiculing the American fundamentalist, or dealing with and woefully misunderstanding the relations between the Italian Government and the Vatican, but *The New Statesman* does not fill more than half its columns with specificially anti-Catholic matter. It will take anti-Catholicism for granted, of course, in everything, because the editor and the readers have never heard of anything else, but it will print matter from a Catholic pen so long as that pen does not present a specifically Catholic plea. It has printed many essays of my own, though sometimes a little doubtful about them when I showed the indirect effects of a culture with which its readers were unfamiliar. I remember one most amusing discussion as to whether I should or should not be allowed to say that *Le Misanthrope* of Molière and Seville cathedral were the two summits of achievement in Western art. This statement in one of my essays was not objected to because it was specifically Catholic—nor was it; any Catholic is free to think Seville hideous and *Le Misanthrope* negligible—it was objected to because it sounded bizarre—just as praise of John Bunyan would have sounded bizarre to the Court of Louis XIV.

The anti-Catholic Press around us is what men call today "subconsciously" anti-Catholic. It would not be possible for the Catholic Press of which I speak to be "subconsciously" Catholic, for Catholicism sticks out, and Catholicism knows a great deal too much of its own motives. But it would deal with matters at large without, at any rate, that overt reference to an especial position which has hitherto been the mark of all our journals.

The first and most obvious answer to the question "What should we add to our existing Catholic Press?" is a daily newspaper like any one of those scores of daily newspapers on the continent of Europe which take Catholic ethics for granted and have the Catholic central vision of national and international affairs.

We must rule that out. Such a daily paper is not possible. It might be possible to have a daily newspaper Catholic in the sense in which our Catholic Press is already Catholic; that is, dealing mainly with specifically Catholic things; but it would not be possible to found and maintain a daily newspaper which would be generally Catholic in tone. The thing has often been talked of; it has never been done, because the only conditions under which it could be done are absent.

Those conditions may change. I speak only of things as they are. The conditions which make a daily paper of this sort impossible are the habits of people in this country in the matter of their daily Press. The kind of thing which the English reader demands of his daily paper makes it a thing which our small poor and scattered body could not afford. An Englishman's daily paper must contain a great deal of matter, the quality being of little consequence; it must be well printed on good paper; it must be delivered very promptly over very wide areas. All this means today an enormous initial capital of some millions and a correspondingly gigantic annual *loss* unless the paper obtains a circulation of very many hundreds of thousands and a corresponding revenue from the advertisers.

It is as certain as anything can be, that, as things are, no paper with a Catholic tone about it, however indirect, could enjoy those advantages. The same forces which make our average daily paper the despicable thing it is would prevent a daily paper informed by the high culture and sane morals of Catholicism from keeping afloat. If, or when, the customs of Englishmen so changed that they would accept first-rate matter, though printed on a few flimsy sheets, as Frenchmen, Germans and Italians accept it, then we could have a Catholic daily paper; but so long as they demand what they do demand for their morning reading, your daily paper of general interest, but of Catholic morals and outlook, cannot live.

There remains the review—monthly, quarterly or weekly.

Here also we are heavily handicapped by national custom. To begin with, the setting up of type is what is called today in this country a "naturally protected" occupation. There is nothing very mysterious or difficult about it; the working of a type-setting machine was learnt in a few days (some people have told me "in a few hours") during the general strike; but the terror in which English capitalists now stand of organized proletarian resistance gives to the naturally protected craft organizations the power to receive the wages they demand. They act as they have been trained to act by capitalist society, which denies the doctrine of the Just Price, which proclaims work to be an evil and the goal of human endeavor to be the avoidance of it; which puts it up as an ideal that individuals should get as much money as they possibly can out of their fellows by any means in their power.

Paper does not come under the same restrictions as printing, but transport does, and much more important than any of these causes in handicapping the weekly or monthly review is, again, the standard in size and outward appearance which public taste demands. You must sell 10,000 copies of a review a week, or rather more, and you must have a solid advertisement revenue as well, to make a weekly review pay. Even so, you must charge double what would be charged in more fortunate countries. A review representing Catholic ideas, but dealing with general matters at large, appearing weekly and costing, say, sixpence, would certainly lose money.

But here comes in a very interesting consideration. *Need* such a paper pay?

That is the main question I would pose here. In my judgment we should not expect nor aim at a profit, and to make a profit a condition of continuance is to doom such a venture from the outset.

In my judgment the failure in the past of all such experiments has been due to an absence of subsidy. It has been taken for granted that a literary and political review of this sort must show a profit or must cease to be. But no one of the anti-Catholic literary and critical reviews would show a profit unless it had an advertisement subsidy. It only gets that advertisement subsidy by being in touch with the anti-Catholic atmosphere in which it lives and in which the readers live, and in which the advertisers live. Had it another tone about it, it would be suspect because it would be reckoned odd, and the advertisement subsidy would not be forthcoming.

I shall be told at this point, by practical men in the advertising trade, that they care nothing for opinions, only for circulation. I don't agree. I have seen too many examples to the contrary. I have witnessed, for instance, the early days of the *Daily*

Herald, when it was a genuinely socialist organ and not the official thing it has become. Its circulation warranted a larger advertisement revenue than it obtained; and the same was true of my own review, "The Eye Witness," which exposed the politicians of the Marconi scandal.

We shall not get enough advertisement subsidy to float us. Therefore, I maintain, the subsidy must be provided from some other source. In other words, we shall never have an efficient Catholic Press of the particular kind I am now envisaging unless there be guaranteed support to make up the inevitable loss.

How large would such a subsidy have to be? For a weekly paper properly staffed and paying proper prices to its contributors, at least £5,000 a year.

In that figure is the answer to the question I have proposed myself. If, or when, a subsidy on that scale can be maintained, there will appear an English literary and critical review which will be of the highest value to the nation; but without the clear understanding that a loss must be faced, and a loss of that magnitude, we shall have either nothing or a series of those failures in the future which will continue our failures of the past. And with this very practical conclusion I would end the first part of these remarks.

But there is a second part. Suppose the thing be done; suppose the guarantee obtained and the loss deliberately envisaged. What machinery should be set up for the creation and maintenance of such an organ? I submit the following conditions:

(i) First, that the guarantors of the fund be as numerous as possible. The advantage of numbers does not lie in the opportunity it gives for a larger amount of money so much as in the opportunity they deny of interference with the machinery of the journal. Where one rich man stands the loss upon an experimental review he is always the master; and as he will not be at the pains of editing (for rich men have something better to do with their time), that means double control and failure. Every paper appealing to educated men is made by its editor. An editor whose own salary

and whose pay list for others is guaranteed by a group is more or less independent. An editor whose finances come from a patron is a servant; and not even the servant of a man who is capable of giving definite orders, but a servant who has to provide all the initiative and yet suffer perpetual interference. Where the bulk of the money comes from one man, or even where two or three wealthy men are the main guarantors, there is still difficulty. It is essential that the fund should come from a number.

(ii) Next, the sums annually subscribed must be prepaid. You must start at the beginning of each year with a sum equivalent to the anticipated loss and a margin over. You must have that capital ready by you. Otherwise the thing falls into the grip of worry, and worry in the organization of a newspaper is like sand in the bearings of a machine; it checks and slows down everything and at last brings disaster.

It would be unwise to use any considerable portion of such a fund for advertising the paper. A paper of this kind is its own advertisement. The old green *Westminster Gazette,* which was far the best literary, critical and political paper of its day, would have retained its place and prestige and such circulation as it had (not very large I am told), even if it had not advertised at all.

(iii) There would have to be some sort of council or small body, not for the running of the paper—it is fatal for such a body to interfere—but for consultation with the editor, and, when his contract should have expired (one would have to begin with at least a five-year contract), for the renewal of it or the finding of another editor. Upon the editor chosen, the moral success of the paper would depend. To a financial success it would by definition be indifferent. And it is a fairly good rule, when you have your editor and he is giving the results you demand, to keep him; for everything in a newspaper of the cultivated sort depends upon personality and unity. The choice of the right editor would be vital. He had better not be elderly; he must have training

in the business; it is most unlikely that you would find such a man among the authors and one chance in a hundred that you would find him in a profession not literary. You should look for him among the daily journalists.

(iv) Here I must add an unusual clause which may be thought paradoxical. There should be no doctrinal control. A review of this kind would not be specifically Catholic. If one made it so it would lose its whole point, and if things appearing in it were subject to a censorship it would cease to be what it was. One would have to trust to the general editorial spirit for one's results, leaving criticism to the correspondence column or to the results on circulation.

(v) There should be in the *format* and make-up of the paper and almost in its constitution a very large department for correspondence.

There, I take it, are the main conditions under which the thing should come into existence. They are sufficiently hard, and in the opinion of many they will render the whole idea fantastic. I do not say that the thing is feasible; I do not say that a large guarantee fund is obtainable. All I say is that those are the conditions under which such a paper could exist and that if they are not observed the experiment will fail. If the guarantors aim at profit, if they are few in number, if they interfere with editorial control, it would have been better not to have launched the thing at all. It would be wasting money instead of spending it on a good object.

But is the object a good one? Would a literary and political review of this kind in modern England be first-rate, and if it came into existence, would it do good to the Catholic cause and to the national cause?

I should answer all those questions in the affirmative, and without hesitation.

Not only would such a review be first-rate, but it would be altogether superior to the ruck of anti-Catholic stuff with which we now have to put up. We are small in numbers, but intellectually we are an élite, and we not only have—out of all proportion to our numbers—men available for the best work, but we have a large margin of indifference and sympathy on which to draw. The journal I have in mind would in a dozen ways express what masses of the educated classes agree with or, at any rate, desire to see stated, and what today they do not see stated. The mere fact that it was not dependent upon an advertisement subsidy would emancipate it; the fact that it had right morals informing it would make it a palatable exception to the stuff upon which we are now fed by the neo-pagan Press of the intellectuals.

Take the attitude of such a review towards the fiction of the moment. All the anti-Catholic critical writing condones or accepts enormities, but in so doing it is not in tune with the best opinion of our time. Reaction against thoroughly bad morals, not only in sexual things, but in other departments of activity, is demanded by an existing and powerful section of general opinion. It is not provided. Or take the effect of a sound international point of view. Today we get nothing but a sort of conventional anti-Catholic litany, an unceasing stream of abuse and misquotation directed against the Catholic side of Europe. It is very wearisome, very futile, and in matters of policy dangerously misleading. We never get Europe presented as it is. The half dozen major problems of international policy turn upon religious culture, and the most important of them upon the conflict between the Catholic and the anti-Catholic culture in Europe. Educated men want to hear these things at least mentioned; they want discussion of them to be in terms of reality, and they are not satisfied. The demand is not met. We get the Prussian case against Poland by the bushel. Whoever hears the Polish case against Prussia? Yet an educated neutral who is indifferent to either side at least wants to hear both, for the fate of his own country will be affected by the sequel to the present conflict.

Such a review would obviously do good to the non-Catholic world. At present the right view of life is not so much denied as ignored. Men do not come across it. Even in the specialized world of apologetics we Catholic writers stand in the rather ridiculous position of perpetually preaching to the converted.

A thoroughly false piece of history comes out; it is well

reviewed and destroyed by a competent pen in the existing Catholic Press. No one outside the Catholic world sees that review. Had it appeared in a paper of general information the non-Catholic would have seen it; he would have learnt something. With such a review we should teach, and we should teach a society which is not only insufficiently taught but is growing less and less taught every day—and an expansion of learning is one of the prime necessities of our time.

An example of what I mean which struck me very forcibly at the time was the case of GDYNIA. When that new port with its great coming effect on international politics was designed and begun there was no journal in England giving the educated Englishman any knowledge of GDYNIA. The name still remains, after all these years, quite unfamiliar. I visited the place three years ago; I wrote on it in one of the monthly reviews; I have seen slight allusions to it here and there, but it has never got into the consciousness of the educated public, because GDYNIA is Polish and Poland is Catholic. A journal such as that which I am describing would not exaggerate the chances of growth in Poland, simply because Poland is Catholic; but it would not leave out things essential to a comprehension of Europe, as does all the Press which is anti-Catholic in tone.

Perhaps the best effect of all which such a journal would have, would be its effect upon the Catholic body itself. It would provide an arena for controversy, it would strengthen the confidence of Catholics, it would instruct them, it would provide them with material, and it would be an introduction of it to the non-Catholic body outside.

Having said all this, I must end by repeating what has, I am sure, run through the reader's mind, if he has had the patience to follow me so far: I mean, that this goal is very difficult of attainment. I should not quarrel too much with the decision that it is even impossible of attainment. But I have noticed in the course of forty years' examination (it is rather more than forty years), since I first became mixed up with journalism and the survey of contemporary things, that: *first,* things one would have thought impossible sometimes come off; *second,* it is the totally unexpected which arrives. The imaginary review of which I have been speaking may appear, after all. More likely something else will appear doing the same work in a quite unexpected fashion.

Science As The Enemy Of Truth

Science cannot be opposed to truth, for it is no less than a part of truth itself, as discovered in a particular sphere. But those who practice physical science may have a corporate spirit which is warped, opposed to true philosophy and therefore to beauty and to goodness. That is exactly what has happened in the development of physical science and of the so-called "scientific" criticism of documents during the last two centuries. The misfortune has happened because the advance in scientific method came after the break-up of Europe and of our common religion. The Process is now reaching its climax in an effort to persuade men against the belief in a beneficent conscious omnipotent Creator, the moral sense and the freedom of the will.

10

SCIENCE AS THE ENEMY OF TRUTH

I

"Science is the enemy of Truth."

That sentence reads absurdly, for it is a direct contradiction in terms.

The definition of science is: "A body of facts ascertained to be true by proof such that we cannot admit their opposite." Thus the fact that water boils when we subject it to heat is a piece of science. The fact that man must have air to breathe if he is to live is also as much a piece of science as the most complicated or the newest result of chemical research.

The word "Science" today is commonly used, and will be used here, in the more restricted sense, as meaning the body of ascertained fact relating to the physical world; to the behavior and history of animate and inanimate objects. The word "scientific" will be extended from physical science to the exact scrutiny of documents, to the examination of records, political and social, and to the critical analysis of literary remains.

The whole point, then, of science being that it is a body of ascertained truth, manifestly the assertion that "Science is the enemy of Truth" makes nonsense.

Yet many men today would by implication at least show their agreement with that phrase, "Science is the enemy of Truth"; and the number of those who feel this more or less consciously is increasing. On seeing a passage beginning, "Science has proved..." or "There is no scientific evidence for..." or

"Examined in a strictly scientific spirit..." and so forth, men are becoming more and more predisposed to quarrel with what follows. They are filled with an "I know all about that!" feeling. On hearing of some method that it is "Scientific" they are at once prepared to find it leading to ridiculous conclusions. They do not feel instructed; they feel warned. Habits of eating, clothing and everything else suggested in the name of "Science" they constantly discover to be inhuman, degrading or simply silly. The term "Scientific" applied to some recommended habit is beginning to have something grotesque about it, as likely to be in opposition to the general conclusions of mankind and our human common sense. As for the name "Scientist," it has fallen on the worst fate of all. It is becoming something of an Aunt Sally, and to call a man a Scientist is perilously near making a laughing-stock of him; unless you add the word "distinguished," which turns him into a statue.

Further, this word "Science" and its derivatives is beginning to be associated with unreliability. The high priests of science yesterday loudly affirmed as eternal truth what today they have to be silent upon because it has been proved false. Yet the new supplanting doctrine is as loudly affirmed today as was the discredited one yesterday—and as it will itself be denied again tomorrow.

Under the influence of such experiences, although few men will as yet pronounce the words, "Science is the enemy of Truth," yet more and more men practically agree with that statement in their emotions. More and more are they associating the word "Science" and its derivatives with the idea of being bamboozled, or annoyed, or presented with incomprehensible absurdities or with truths solemnly affirmed to be eternal and yet bursting at frequent intervals, or with what is manifestly contrary to experience. Now, what is manifestly opposed to experience, or absurd, or unstable is clearly at issue with Truth.

Yet I say again, the phrase "Science is the enemy of Truth," is a contradiction in terms.

How, then, has this state of mind arisen? Why can one write down with the certitude of receiving so much hearty, though often only indirect, agreement, "Science is the enemy of truth"?

To understand the matter let us write down another simple phrase:

"Drink is the enemy of health."

Here is a phrase to which millions of men and women will give enthusiastic support. Yet on the face of it this phrase also is a contradiction in terms. Health is a term signifying the perfect physical functioning of the human body. Drinking is a term signifying the absorption of liquid by the human body. But to the functioning of the human body at all, let alone perfectly, absorption of liquid is essential. Man must drink to live, let alone to keep his health. Men kept from drinking, as shipwrecked sailors are, die mad in a short time. How, then, can you say: "Drink is the enemy of health"?

To those who would object to the phrase the reply would come at once: "You know well enough what I mean; the drinking of stimulants is the enemy of health." But to this reply, in turn, will come the answer: "Not so; we have all known masses of people who drank wine and beer regularly, and were perfectly healthy."

To which would come the further answer: "Yes; you do know what I mean. I mean that the drinking of stimulants to excess is the enemy of health."

So there we have it. All language is shorthand; any sentence to express reality must be modified indefinitely; and so it is with the sentence: "Science is the enemy of Truth."

For this let us write, "The Modern Scientific Spirit is the enemy of Truth," and we shall have it pat. The modern scientific spirit as applied to daily practice, to life, and to letters, and, above all, to religion, is the enemy of truth.

This is my thesis, and very important it is. The Modern Scientific Spirit being the enemy of truth, is the enemy of right living and of human happiness, and if it is not tackled, humbled and set right, will lead us to misery.

II

The Modern Scientific Spirit may be defined as the practice of Science under a false philosophy; that is, the research and establishment of ascertainable facts in the physical world *but* the application of those facts in an irrational and perverted mood. In other words, the Modern Scientific Spirit is always looking for, and finding, facts in order to misuse them.

Begin by remarking an important historical point; the increased interest in physical science which has been the mark of modern times and the increasing use of what are called "scientific methods" in the writing of history and in the critical examination of literary documents, did not produce the false philosophy under which it now works and which is doing all the harm. It found the false philosophy well launched, fell under its influence when young, and has remained captured by it ever since.

In Science, physical, documentary, or of any other kind, there cannot be inherently a false philosophy, for truth does not contradict truth. Mankind has been at Science since men have been men, and within their limited range the animals are practicing science all day long. A bird which gives up at last the attempt to fly through a glass window has arrived through experiment and conclusion at the fact that the glass is not penetrable by him and ceases to entertain the idea of the opposite. The burnt child who dreads the fire has done a little work in Science, so has the whole human race in its tremendous achievement of our original civilization, which is incomparably greater, in extent as well as in quality, than the added results of the last few generations. Whoever first cooked meat, or first framed something like a plow, or first carved an image, was doing a bit of scientific work: discovering and establishing fact by experiment and applying that fact to the uses of mankind. There was not and could not be anything of perversion or falsity attached to so necessary, permanent, original and enduring a human process, anymore than there could be to breathing or to sleeping.

In particular, we may note that the chief characteristic in the particular philosophy of the modern scientific spirit, Monism—Doom—is as old as the hills. The denial of Free Will in the universe, the subjecting of all happenings to necessary fate, was not begun by modern biology. It was a perverted mood into which men tended to fall from the earliest recorded times; and during the break-up of our Christian culture four hundred years ago Calvin was the powerful prophet of it long before anything that can seriously be called "modern" physical experiment began. Spinoza, in another way, was also a prophet of it, long before modern physical research had taken on its later characteristic extension.

And if this is true of the chief error, it is true of the accompanying minor errors. Deism (or Pantheism), Rationalism, stand to the development of the modern scientific mood not as children, but as parents. Having gone off the rails of sound philosophy because the social forces around them shepherded them into the wrong way, the pioneers of modern physical science (for the most part) started under these misconceptions and read them into all they did, handing on the tradition to their followers. Bad reasoning and a bad application of what they found were not the product of what they found. They did not (for instance) gradually come to disbelieve in the possibility of miracle because they had proved it impossible by experiment. They disbelieved in it already, before they began experimenting, and were confirmed in their disbelief by observing, with owlish wisdom, that miracles did not commonly take place in the routine of physical cause and effect. They were ready to be confirmed in their mistake, and the particular work in which they were engaged especially lent itself to so confirming them.

III

The capital, the fundamental sin of method (not of creed) in what we call the Modern Scientific Spirit, is the substitution of Numerical Synthesis for Integration.

Other accompanying errors of method allied to and in particular proceeding from this capital error shall be noted; but before proceeding to them it is necessary to explain the terms used and to show why the substitution of Numerical Synthesis for Integration as a method of arriving at truth is calamitous, and, far from leading one to truth, debars one from attaining it.

We mean by integration that faculty in the human mind whereby it is able to combine an indefinitely large number of impressions (colloquially we say: "an *infinite* number of impressions") in order to arrive at reality.

For instance, if a man seeing another man coming towards him along a path says: "Here comes my friend, Brown," he is quite certain of the truth of what he says, and he is right to be certain. His mind has not created an image, but appreciated an external object, and his judgment is coincident with that object.

But he has not noted every detail characteristic of Brown. He has not cataloged one by one the gestures and the gait, the elements of the contours and all the rest of it. He has received an indefinitely large number of indefinitely small impressions and combined them, without addition, into one immediate whole.

It is the same with a taste, with a color, with the recognition of anything. A man sees the truth that a distant vessel is of such and such a rig, if he is familiar with that rig, though the indications, if he were to set them down, would seem each individually quite insufficient, and even any sum of them insufficient. Or take what is perhaps the most lucid example of all, the recognition of a type of tree. A man looking at a tree a good way off says with complete certainty, if he is acquainted with such trees: "That is an oak." He cannot see the individual leaves, and if he did he would be a great fool to go over them one by one and not be sure of his oak until he had examined them all. He would be a great fool if he went on to say: "Well, the leaves seem to be all right; but now I must look closely at the bark and I must have a section of the grain, and what about the shape of the boughs?" He, as we say, "knows an oak tree when he sees one." And that "knowing" is a process of integration. It is the immediate combining of an indefinitely large number of indefinitely small indications into one short flash of communion with reality.

The metaphor of "Integration," the best I know in this connection, is taken from mathematics, in which science the word "Integration" is used of arriving at a result through the consideration of what are called "infinitesimals"; an infinitely great number of which, for instance, give the formula of a curve.

This God-given faculty of Integration is the just and only method of perception we possess: I mean, of perception sufficient to bring us into touch with reality and to recognize a thing. It is our only way of truth. We use it in every moment of our lives, and in proportion to our vigor in using it are we sane.

Integration lies at the basis, not only of our recognizing things, but of our judgment upon character and events. Thus, we say that one man "is of good judgment," because he integrates well, though he may not be able to give reasons for his judgment; and another man "of bad judgment," because he integrates badly, although he piles up reasons and calculations over much. Hence, also, we say that good judgment is based upon experience, and hence do we rightly mistrust a man's judgment in practical affairs—other things being equal—when he is inexperienced in the particular matter involved, however well he knows the theory of the business.

Now, the Modern Scientific Spirit has more and more fettered itself with a different, false and almost contradictory method of arriving at truth.

It adds together numerically a comparatively small number of ascertained truths with regard to any object and then propounds its conclusion, as though by possession of these few gross certainties it had a sufficient basis for that conclusion. What is more, it very impudently puts forward such a conclusion against the sound conclusion arrived at by the powers of integration present in the common man.

I shall never forget a personage of my early youth who gave us boys lectures in chemistry (for the honor of my old school I must say that it was not at this school that they were given). He came out one day with this enormity: "A diamond is therefore" (Oh, glorious "therefore"!) "the same thing as a lump of coal." Why, a man might go to jail for pretending that they were the same thing! A diamond is *not* a lump of coal, and a lump of coal is *not* a diamond. The Science of this lecturer was the enemy of Truth.

Upon one line of analysis, insofar as the gentleman in question had knowledge, a lump of coal gave the same results as a diamond. They both, along that one line of analysis, presented themselves as what he called "carbon"; and "carbon" was what he called an "element," and an element consisted of hypothetical "molecules," in which there was but one kind of hypothetical "atoms." The atoms he was quite sure were atoms of carbon, and *therefore* (Oh, glorious "therefore"!) the diamond and the carbon, whose difference stared him in the face, were the same thing. But we infants knew very well they were not the same thing. Nor are they the same thing. Though most of us were of the middle class, we had seen diamonds—and with coal we were all familiar. We had done our little integrations in these affairs, and we knew that a man who could call a lump of coal a diamond would call cricket, football. Along one line of analysis cricket and football are both games. Along another they are both played with a ball. Along another they are both of English origin. In each case "Experiment on independent lines confirms the hypothesis of identity." Nevertheless, to affirm identity between them is to talk rubbish.

The Modern Scientific Spirit is at war with common sense and with universal judgment—that is with truth—principally because it has fallen into this false method. But there are many other allied errors in method which it commits.

It is perpetually presenting hypothesis for fact. In the matter of interpreting (not establishing) documents the whole of the Higher Criticism is a mass of that. Three quarters of the terminology of modern chemistry is a mass of that, and modern geology reeks with it. It was not so long ago—a lifetime at most—we were told, not as an hypothesis, but as a fact, that the earth was a molten mass with a thin crust, upon which we walked about precariously, as on an egg-shell, the boiling stuff bursting out at volcanoes. It was an hypothesis to explain many evident phenomena, including the increase of heat with depth, but it was only an hypothesis—yet it was put forward as an ascertained truth. Today the "scientific" earth is fairly solid. Tomorrow it may be hollow.

Again, the Modern Scientific Spirit revels in false authority; that is, in substituting for proof assertion backed by a name. I have under my hand as I write a very amusing little instance of this. Common sense reasonably presumes from tradition, from a knowledge of how books are made, from an appreciation of the tone and sincerity of the writer and so forth, that the Acts of the Apostles were written by one man, a companion of St. Paul, and that companion St. Luke, the author of the Gospel. Yet I find seriously given, as a sufficient rebuttal to this process of integration, the following formidable roll-call of gentlemen, "Hilgenfeld, Holtzmann, Overbeck, Hansrath, Weizsacher, Wendt, Schürer, Pfleiderer, von Soden, Spitta, Jülicher, J. Weiss, Knopf, Clemen, Konigsmann, De Wette, Baur, and Zeller." I know nothing of their work; I do no more than copy a list from a received text book, but it is a typical list. I am asked to believe the Acts of the Apostles to be a mixture of forgery and patchwork, and when I ask for rational proofs I am given a magic formula of oracles. It is no good saying that all these worthies have labored. I'm sure they have—too much. The point is that this citation of mere names *is* the common form of Science today, and on it we are expected to pin our faith—in the irrational.

Again, the Modern Scientific Spirit, you will be distressed to hear, is perpetually using the same word in two senses, one of the commonest errors into which dolts have always fallen. An excellent example of this is the use of the word "Natural Selection" to mean two totally different things.

(a) The undoubted truth that adverse conditions tend to kill off a type and favorable conditions tend to continue it.

(b) The creative power of this process accounting for all organic differentiation.

Thus, a biologist of repute at Oxford, having been challenged for an actual case of Natural Selection in the second sense, gave the instance of black moths which lived side by side with white moths in a certain wood. The trees of the wood were dark pines; with the result that the white moths had a bad time, being easily picked off, while the black moths flourished. But when the trees of the wood were gradually replaced by light colored birch trees, it was the other way about; the white moths flourished and the black moths diminished. Surely it hardly needed great learning to expect such a result! But the Scientist mixed up that obvious result with a totally different thing, to wit, *the turning of the black moths into white moths* through the new birch plantation. That was what he had to give an instance of, and he thought in his muddled way that what he did give was on all fours with the instance required of him.

Indeed, this use of the term in two different senses during the same argument is repeated constantly, as when you get the word "health" used to mean now what it normally means, and again, *what it may connote, but does not necessarily connote,* longevity. As in the phrase: "The climate was thought unhealthy, but *scientific observation* has shown that the death rate is lower than in surrounding districts."

We have another even more common example of it in the dreadful muddle with the word "creation," as in the phrase: "Modern Science has made the idea of creation inconceivable, for *we now know* that living organisms *invariably* proceed from other living organisms." Mark the mixture of ignorance and indolence in a sentence like that and admire the foison [abundance] of folly in it! It uses the word "creation" in two quite distinct senses, to wit, mediate and immediate creation, as though the two were identical. It affirms that we know what we don't know and perhaps never shall know. It ascribes to a powerful Mumbo-Jumbo called "Modern Science" a marvelous new discovery which has been a commonplace with the whole human race from immemorial time—the fact that in general experience you only get chickens from eggs.

The Modern Scientific Spirit revels in unproved and unexplained postulates; as in the case of Renan, who at the opening of his book on the history of the children of Israel (I quote from memory) tells us point blank that the human race did not arise at one place but in many. The postulate that physical cause and effect must follow the same process in any place and at any time runs through the whole of modern scientific assertion. It is reasonable enough, but neither is it self-evident nor is demonstration attempted. It is admitted, of course, that all proof must have its postulates. You always come back at last to something which must be held and cannot be proved. But even so, you can and should give reasons why you hold it, although those reasons are not of the nature either of experimental or deductive proof. But nine times out of ten your Modern Scientist puts forward his postulates, by implication at least, in circular fashion, basing them upon the conclusions drawn from them. For instance, he postulates that light behaves outside this world as it behaves here. But his confidence is based upon experiment made here. The least he could do would be to say: "I postulate—for I cannot prove it—that light follows the same laws under non-terrestrial conditions as it follows under these conditions—where alone I experience it." But he hardly ever does that. Huxley was great enough to do it, but Huxley was exceptional. The run of modern Scientific writing takes its form of faith for granted and does not even know that it is a faith.

Yet another error, and one exceedingly common in the action of the Modern Scientific Spirit, is the confusion of categories; and a bad mark of stupidity it is, since the chief mark of intelligence is the distinction of categories.

For instance, there is that perpetually recurrent error of confusing proof with analogy, as when the scientist tells you that a general similarity of body-structure in different animals proves a common ancestor. Then there is confusion of certitude in one process with certitude in another; for instance, the confusion between certitude in a mathematical identity with certitude in an observed physical phenomenon, as when a man says that we are "as certain the earth is round as that two and two make four." There is also confusion between the categories of things immediately observed and things inferred, giving to the last the same degree of certitude as to the first; as when one confidently assures you that a prehistoric being of whom he has but a handful of broken bones carried on like a known contemporary savage.

There is the error of regarding a long chain of hypothetical conclusions as equivalent in strength to the best established link in the chain, instead of the strength of the weakest link—and so on. But the worst error after that original sin of substituting numerical synthesis for integration is the closely allied error of assuming universal knowledge.

Now, this folly will, I know, be indignantly denied in a chorus by all those who commit it. As for assuming universal knowledge, they profess themselves to be groping from one ascertained truth to another; to be of all men the most ready to admit their ignorance of what is not in their province, and the immensity of the field still remaining for exploration.

Of course, they are not conscious of their error; if they were they could be cured of it. But see how they go to work! One will tell you that a bottle of Richebourg of 1921 (such as may be drunk with profit in the Three Pheasants at Dijon) is *"the equivalent"* of a flask of whisky, because the "alcoholic content" is the same; presupposing so universal a knowledge as can put in their right order of importance all the other things in which the two liquids differ, leaving the "alcoholic content" the outstanding mark. Another will tell you that the climate of one place which makes you ill *must* be the same as the climate of another (in which you thrive), because all our existing means of measurement give us similar results for the two in heat and cold and damp and barometrical pressure and the rest of it. This is to presuppose that there are no other elements in climate which we cannot measure, or that if they exist they are unimportant because we cannot measure them. It is to presuppose that the speaker knows all there is to know in the matter of climate.

IV

In social practice the fruits of a false philosophy are more important than the false philosophy itself. The greed, ugliness and vice of a Calvinist town affect us in practice more than a misstatement on Election and Efficient Grace. So the mischief done by the Modern Scientific Spirit is most felt, not in its errors of reasoning, but in the established school or fashion under which its exponents are molded. The exponents and imposers of that Spirit bear certain unmistakable characteristics throughout the modern world, and one knows them for what they are as one knows a jockey or a prize fighter; they are one kind. To point out that there are exceptions: that many of them have humor: that some even are capable of doubting whether they are so certain, after all: that great names among them are even of a kind quite opposite from the general run, does not contradict the truth that they form a general body, and almost a corporation.

There is nothing extraordinary about this. What is extraordinary is that it should not be yet fully recognized, though I think it is being more and more recognized as time goes on. There have always been fashions or schools of this sort. There have always arisen in the group of learned professions a corresponding group of characteristics, of underlying presumptions in thought, of effects on conduct, which have no necessary connection with the subject studied. Thus, your classical scholar in one university has his mark, "the stamp of the trade," your classical scholar in a foreign university will have perhaps a somewhat different mark, but a mark of the same species.

For, indeed, Classical Scholarship as the Renaissance advanced, developed a certain body with which to clothe its soul. One may curiously inquire how it is that a wide and precise reading in the dead languages produces these characteristics, just as I shall shortly examine why certain characteristics in the average modern scientist have arisen; but one must everywhere recognize that these *are* concrete attributes not directly connected with the abstract functions of a trade, but standing to it as clothing does to the body.

In the case of the Classical Scholar a few of these outward characteristics may be evil, some of them are rather ridiculous, but most of them are estimable, and many of them excite our ardent and just admiration. It is evil in him to think scholarship greater than virtue; it is ridiculous in him to exaggerate the importance of making false quantities in Latin. It is estimable in him to have so much taste; it is most admirable to be filled with the profound and vivifying culture which the Classics alone can give—for it is impossible to be steeped in the great works which lie at the roots of our civilization and not be enlarged and nourished thereby. But the corporate marks of the modern Scientific exponent are *not,* for the most part, admirable.

What is admirable in him are not marks peculiar to his corporation. One is accuracy in detail. Another is industry. Another devotion to the research undertaken. Another is candor: an error having been committed, it is always acknowledged in what is called the "Scientific world"; further experiment, modifying what has been hitherto accepted, is not usually boycotted. Though there is necessarily jealousy among scientists, as there always will be among the members of the same profession, there is more generosity than in most callings. And the last and by far the finest in this list of the better characteristics in our Scientists is an indifference to wealth, such as you may find, indeed, in most men absorbed in any occupation, but particularly here. There are exceptions, but they are rare. It is almost a commonplace that the robbers of finance can prey at will on the Scientist, and it is to the honor of the Scientist that it should be a commonplace.

Unfortunately there are many other less admirable characteristics which very strongly mark the Scientific corporation as a whole. I think it will be of interest to catalog some of these *seriatim.*

First, I remark a set of characteristics in them exactly corresponding to what the Scientists themselves used to denounce as "priestcraft"; what may be called the "Mumbo-jumbo" group—and Heaven knows it applies a great deal more to the scientists than it ever did to the priests of any false religion.

Part of this is the "Superior information" business: telling the layman that he cannot follow the difficult process by which a result has been arrived at, and that therefore he must take it on trust. There is also something of an hieratic language, but of a very undignified type: litanies of words barbarously compounded from Latin and Greek, sometimes in a mixture of the two with the vernacular. Part of this is no doubt necessary; one must have technical terms, one cannot be forever explaining. Still, there is a very damnable plague of what plain people call "long words."

There is also the Marvel. Here the scientist has a most powerful instrument, the more powerful that it does not pretend to depend—as in the old Pagan priestcraft—upon an irrational process, but upon methods which anyone can use if he will give up his time to them. The Scientist will be forever showing us that things are not what they seem, expatiating upon the astonishing character of Scientific achievement. Thus, I read in a book which has sold by scores of thousands under the name of a chief scientific authority in the department of physics, that the hypothetical "electron" is "at once everywhere and nowhere"—and this nonsense is swallowed whole by people who smile at the mystery of the Trinity.

Even as I write, my daily paper publishes the conclusion of a Scientist that after accurate measurement of sound he can show the London of Motor Buses and the Pneumatic Drill to be a haven of quiet compared to the old London of Hansom Cabs.

From this solemn hieratic humbug, comes the habit of speaking of fellow pundits in terms of reverence and awe, calling upon us outsiders to worship them, ascribing to them all manner of rare virtues, and even, when things go wrong, dubbing them "martyrs."

There is by the way no more absurd example of "Scientific" Mumbo-jumbo than this last. A "martyr to science" should properly mean one who bears witness to scientific truth by submitting to suffering rather than recant his conviction. In this sense men are indeed martyrs to scientific truth who sufficiently anger the Scientists by pointing out their mistakes. Samuel Butler in his day was a martyr to science, in that he suffered for being a pioneer in challenging the folly of the Darwinians. But our new priesthood does not use the word "martyr" in this sense at all. They apply it to a man who is blown up in the course of a chemical experiment, or who dies of a disease caught in a medical one. And as for "the gulf between clergy and laity," which was made such a grievance of against real priests; it is nothing to the gulf between the ignorant herd and Scientific Persons. They show a corporate and almost universal contempt for the man who has not had the leisure to go through all their studies, but who can bring valid criticism to bear on their laughable conclusions; they do not meet his criticism in its own field, they appeal to Status, to their own necessary and unapproachable superiority.

I have found that very horribly true in my own department of history. Your "Scientific" historian having concentrated on one tiny section, on which he has become, he believes, an expert—at the expense of all other knowledge—is always disdainful of, and sometimes furious against, the man with a wide range of general knowledge, who is properly equipped for exposing the expert's absurdities. Thus, I have known not a few specialists in medieval documents who have argued by the volume on the size of the Virgate, and who had no idea what a team could plow in a day and even (what is really monstrous) were ignorant of what is meant by the word "fallow." I have found an expert in other medieval documents who assured me that a city—a city of the fourteenth century—with half as many parish churches as London, with walls three miles round, and so crammed full of people that it had burst out into suburbs beyond those walls, had less than six thousand people living in it. The other experts were all with him. How did they fall into such nonsense? By divorce from common sense and relying on a document. There happened to have survived one fragmentary parchment which it was imagined gave a full list of the male inhabitants of over fourteen years of age in one district. On that basis was the myth built. When it was pointed out that a list comprising all males over fourteen would have the same surnames repeated over and over again, and that this list did not show such repetition, they boggled. The "Scientific" mind was astonished to hear that unless surnames are frequently repeated in such a list it *cannot* be a complete list of males.

Not a long time ago, when the scientists were still talking about an imaginary stuff called ether, they gave it qualities which were contradictory and the sum of which made arrant nonsense. It was, as a great man has well said, no more than "the nominative of the verb to vibrate." But when the plain man pointed out that they were talking nonsense, how angry they were! They must be glad, I think, to have scrapped the thing. It was high time.

They suffer from a fatuous glory in perpetual revelation and ceaselessly proclaim to the common man hidden treasures suddenly revealed—discoveries with which their unfortunate audience have already been familiar for a lifetime.

The best example, I think, of this is the original and still prolonged scientific attack upon the Gospel of St. John; which we are solemnly assured is quite different in tone and manner from the Synoptic Gospels. We are bidden to open our eyes to this revelation, to rejoice in the new and dazzling light—whereas I suppose there was not one of us, though he might not know any language but his own and might have read but half a dozen books outside his Testament, who could not find out for himself in ten minutes that the tone and style of the Gospel of St. John is different from that of the Synoptics.

But there are plenty of other instances. It is only the other day that in the department of chemistry a great authority announced to the world in clarion tones that profound research had proved margarine to be less nutritious than butter.

Yet another scientific authority, after duly making the experiment upon a dozen selected typists (male typists let us hope!), announced his discovery that a little "alcohol," as he called it (I will bet it was whisky) stimulated them at their work, but a good deal more made them dull and inaccurate, while a still larger dose (he gave it all in decimals of centiliters) rendered them perfectly incapable of typewriting at all.

But apart from the weakness of the Modern Scientific Spirit

in playing at Pontificals, there is a weakness of logic. They mistake accumulation of items, irrespective of weight, for cogency; thus, having found one relic of the past which may or may not be of such and such an age, they argue as though to find thousands of such relics would make the guess at the age more accurate. Again, when they set out to sustain a theory they arrange their evidence in a shamefully irrelevant fashion, which plain reason condemns. In biology and anthropology they are specially guilty of thus manipulating proofs to fit theory, instead of testing hypothesis by experiment, which is their profession.

Not one, but a hundred, first-class authorities on anthropology give us detailed accounts of men's behavior before recorded history began. In most of these accounts man is described as something repulsive, the better to confirm the reader's vanity. In all there is drawn a picture of something which the writer never saw and never knew, his inferences for the making of which are of the flimsiest kind, built, some of them upon conjecture, most of them upon nothing; yet the stuff is put forward as confidently as though it were the description of a real experience, in a contemporary place, of things which the writer himself had seen and heard.

There are innumerable examples of this sort of thing. The late Andrew Lang had plenty of fun with Fraser's *Golden Bough,* and its hypothesis of the "Sacrificed Divinity Royal." He showed how good evidence, doubtful evidence, and no evidence at all were all put on a level, and how the object of the writer was not to judge by evidence between various possibilities, but to force evidence for a preconceived thesis. Indeed the very soul of this exceedingly unscientific sort of science is forcing facts to fit theories; and any theory can be made to look true if you ignore evidence against and arrange the evidence in its favor cumulatively instead of giving it in the order of value. Indeed, the *Golden Bough* is a feast for satire.

I could have shown you some years ago an exhibit in one of our scientific museums where a row of skulls several yards long ran in series like a railway train, from a very flat little thing at one end, which was that of I know not what ape, to a big round thing at the other, which was the skull of I know not what modern criminal or saint. There was a long ladder of gradations in between, so that the whole row proceeded charmingly to the desired end of suggesting that they had come in succession by regular development from first to last. It was most convincing—because the arrangement was artificially made. Had it been naturally made in order of time or of place, or in order of resemblances in the rest of the skeleton, it would have produced a very different effect.

And talking of this, I remember another series abroad, where some typically "Scientific" dealer in comparative religion had set on parade a regiment of little statues, each representing a mother with a child in her arms and ending up with a glorious specimen of Our Lady and the Infant Jesus, a triumph of the thirteenth century. Here again there was the most carefully continuous arrangement, the object being to "prove" that the reverence we pay to the Mother of God was as false as the reverence the most degraded savage had paid to his grotesque fetish. Even had the order been genuine, it would have proved nothing of the kind; it would only have meant that as religion must be expressed in certain symbols there will be something in common between the symbols of the false religion and of the true, and that there is in every false religion, even in that of the materialistic scientist, something of reality. But the order was not genuine; it was artificial and false. Some of the statues had nothing to do with any religion but were natural representatives of a familiar group. Others were from family shrines where the representation of a mother and child would be equally natural. The whole series was not arrayed in order of time or of place but only so as to suggest that the Divine Mother and Child are not divine at all, but man-made—as statues are.

We reverence Our Lady because she is the Supreme Mother, the Mother of the Incarnate Word; and the whole meaning of the Incarnation is that it is human as well as Divine. We represent Our Lady with the Little Lord in her arms in order to emphasize the union of the human and the divine which the historic event called the Incarnation means. A Pagan moved to worship will naturally yearn for a similar union of the human and the Divine, and though he has it not he will symbolize his desire. His desire will call up a phantasm, which in our case is no phantasm, but a reality. All this the scientific gentlemen who artificially arranged the row of statues never allowed for and probably never heard of.

There is one more head to be added (there are many more, but one most important), the Modern Scientific Spirit has lost logic, and so remains blind to proportion and therefore ignorant of essential things. It not only abandons logic, but sneers at it. It has produced in its votaries an open negation of reason, presuming an opposition between logic and reality. It is this abandonment of reason which leaves them contemptuous of theology, the highest intellectual exercise of the human race. And it is through their consequent blindness to scale that the Scientists are contemptuous of the humanities and of exalted things.

Now, if at the end of such a catalog I be told that it is an outrageous caricature (and I am sure I shall be told that), and if in proof that it is a caricature there be named to me one exception after another—a few Modern Scientists who seem to have none of these intellectual failings, some who suffer from certain of them but not from others, and so on—I answer that, by the same process, you could make out any general descriptive category of Professional Character to be false.

Take my own profession, that of letters. It can justly be brought against us writers, and particularly against those of us who wish to be thought poets, that we are vain and touchy, and that we put art before morals. There are plenty of other heads in the indictment against us, but those two are the main ones. They are pretty bad—also they are perfectly true.

It is of no consequence to tell me that poet Brown, now happily dead, was thick-skinned, or that Poet Smith, still living, is humble, or that Poet Jones, rather than offend good morals, destroyed his best work and remained obscure. The truth is true of the mass of them; we have today such a herd of poets caracoling about, and such a vast army of prose writers crowding the marketplace, that we can generalize with certitude; my profession as a whole is vain, touchy, and careless of morals.

So with the exponent of the Modern Scientific Spirit. So with the man who is the typical Modern Scientist. We are always hearing that the *true* Scientist is distinguished for the virtues opposite to those vices which I have just catalogued. The *true* scientist is particularly humble; he never affirms a thing as certain until it is proved beyond the shadow of a doubt, and he always gives his proofs. He never quotes a mere name as authority. Pseudo-scientists and mere popular writers on Science may go on like that, but the *true* scientist doesn't. I am afraid this true scientist is like "Nature's gentleman" and the "moral victory"—the first of which is rarely a gentleman and the second never a victory. The Modern Scientific Spirit is, in the main, as I have described it and its exponents; its priests of lesser and higher degree suffer from those errors in mental attitude, in method, and in intellectual process which make their teaching the enemy of truth.

V

Let us ask ourselves how this tone of mind grew up. What influences were at work to create this lamentable Modern Scientific Spirit? To seek an answer to such a question is of practical utility, for you cannot attempt to remedy an evil until you have understood it, and you cannot understand it until you have some knowledge of its causes.

The causes in this case, being buried in that profound and multiple thing, human character, largely escape us; but some main causes I think we can trace.

First we have the mechanical process which in the case of documentary criticism consists largely in mere counting; and in physics in the mere establishment of regular recurrence.

That the scientific worker should be limited to this tedious and lifeless round is necessary. He should be pitied for being under that servitude, not envied for it, still less admired for its effects upon him. Subjection to such a mechanical round is in the very nature of his trade. It is as inevitable to his work as muddiness is inevitable to a hedger and ditcher. If he could take it humbly, and if the man who is perforce occupied in this mechanical life admits his limitations, no harm is done to him or his readers; on the contrary, he is very useful, he is adding to our stock of knowledge. But if he allows the worst effects of such a life to warp his philosophy the result is ill indeed.

Thus, in the case of the Modern Scientific Spirit applied to documentary investigation we have such examples as the following (let one stand for a thousand):

The writer is setting out to prove the favorite "scientific" thesis that a certain portion of Holy Writ was not set down by one writer, but is a sort of quilt or patchwork in which there are "strata" from various hands—any number of them, so that it be not the natural number *one*.

The critic proceeds as follows:

"In the 480 verses of Chapters I to XII and in Chapter XV there are only 188 words which are not found in the rest of the book and in the corresponding gospel. According to this proportion, only 38 such words should be discoverable in the verses of the 16th, 20th, 21st, 27th and 28th Chapters. But the actual number is three times as many. Again, in the first-named and larger part of the work there are 657 words (excluding proper names) which are wanting in the corresponding gospel. Therefore in the lesser section, which is about one tenth of the whole, we should expect about 66 such words; whereas there are 162, nearly two and a half times as many."

From which solemn piece of elementary numeration it seems that a whole string of so-called authorities have decided that the lesser part of the document proceeded from another hand than the greater part!

Face nonsense of this kind openly and tell me what you think of it? What you will think of it if you have ever written anything creatively yourself I know very well; the idea that a writer always uses the same vocabulary and always in the same proportion is nonsense. But it needs no personal experience in authorship to see what rubbish the whole thing is. Apply the same test to almost any living writer at random and you will see it fail. Besides which, are books, especially vivid books, written as a fact in "strata"? Are they not, must they not be, in the nature of things written by one author? Of course they must! Yet the method has been applied, not only where the object was to destroy the authority of Holy Writ, but where it was only an object to destroy tradition at large. We have been asked to believe that great poems of antiquity were written in this composite fashion. How is it no modern ones were?

With the scientific spirit in physical research there is the same mechanical taint as in documentary criticism, though in this case it is not of its nature ridiculous, and only does harm when it affects the reason. The scientist engaged in physical research must be forever watching identical recurrence of cause and effect, always seeing the same results following upon the same preliminaries. Mechanical habit in this case breeds in him a blindness to the extent of will and of diversity (of which will is the cause) throughout the universe.

It *need* not blind him. He can say to himself: "When I conduct a new experiment, I am only watching what is normal in any natural sequence. It is no new discovery to find such sequence invariable in my new experiments; it is equally invariable in the oldest experiments. Man has known from the beginning that if you threw a stone into the air it would fall to the ground. But that has not prevented him from believing it possible that an occasional miracle might arrest its flight."

I say that the daily habit of watching invariable phenomena *need* not make the mind itself mechanical nor blind to the multiplicity of will, but presumably it tends to do so, especially if it be not corrected by an ambient true philosophy, but predisposed to a false fatalistic one.

Next the scientific practice breeds a habit of certitude which the vulgar would call "cocksureness." The great mass of the results arrived at are certain, demonstrated over and over again, and never failing. There follows a tendency to two particular habits in the mind thus occupied: First, the habit of thinking that certitudes can only be arrived at experimentally; next, that hypotheses, the least certain of things, are themselves certitudes.

If a man deny that two substances which have been named oxygen and hydrogen disappear under some circumstances and that their total mass reappears in a completely different substance, which we call water, he is denying a certitude arrived at by physical science. But if he doubt the theories by which this strange transformation is explained, he is *not* denying a certitude; he is only challenging something of its nature uncertain and saying that the hypothesis should not be put forward as fact. But the man steeped in scientific work easily comes to confuse the one type of denial with the other. He will think that the sensible fellow who challenges the fantasies of theory is doing so from the same blockheadedness as might make a fool challenge ascertained truth. And that is why (as I shall repeat at the conclusion) this essay, if it is read at all, will be called an attack on Science.

Next, your Scientist has acquired a habit of achievement in knowledge: in knowledge not possessed by the mass of other men. This breeds in him a natural pride, and from that root, I think, spreads that extraordinary presupposition I have noted, unconscious, but very much alive, that the scientist is possessed of universal knowledge. Hence I take it [to be] the mood shown in the example of climate which I gave above; the mood which presumes that, when all that can be *measured* by our present instruments and methods is stated, there has been stated all that *exists* in the case.

Next, a cause of the Modern Scientific Spirit's disease would seem to be the exclusion from consciousness of all that is not measurable by known and divisible units; because the scientific method can only deal with results recorded in known and divisible units. Thus, the physical scientist tends through habit to a state of mind in which qualities not so measurable seem negligible or imaginary; hence the loss of the sense of beauty—the loss of all that is qualitative; the loss of distinction and of hierarchy in sensation.

But the last cause of intellectual evil in the Modern Scientific Spirit is different from all of these, and may be thus expressed: *Anyone can, with patience, do scientific work.* It demands no individual, still less any rare, talent. The reward of scientific work in Physics or Record, the fame which it achieves, has nothing to do with the intellectual or creative ability of the man whose name is attached to it.

The result of this is that intellectual ability, critical or creative, will be at a discount among scientists, for fame is in every form of activity a criterion of success. To excel in playing the violin, or in majestic architecture, or in lovely painting, or in verse, you must possess exceptional qualities. Of a thousand men only a few could be taught to paint even fairly beautiful things; perhaps not one in such a number could reach the fame attaching to genius. Of a thousand men only a few can write tolerable verse; not one in a thousand or perhaps in a million will ever write good poetry. But anyone of common mental and physical health can practice scientific research, whether in physics, or biology, or history or literary documents. Anyone can count the number of times in which the word *ingens* occurs in the Aeneid and compare the proportion of its frequency there with some other Latin poem. Anyone can test style by mere number; it takes special talent to savor style, and it takes genius to understand it fully.

Anyone can try by patient experiment what happens if this or that substance be mixed in this or that proportion with some other under this or that condition. Anyone can vary the experiment in any number of ways. He that hits in this fashion on something novel and of use will have fame. He who, having hit upon a series of such things, comes to some very obvious conclusion through the coordination of that series, will also have fame. The fame will be the product of luck and industry. It will not be the product of special talent.

So with the scientific historian. His card indexing of innumerable documentary points will produce *some* results, and from these there *may* emerge an important discovery; but it was not even a *flair* which made the discovery: still less a genius for perception. It was not a talent for visualizing the past, it was not a profound understanding of human nature by which he could explain some happening, it was nothing more, intellectually, than is the setting up of ninepins in a row or the pricking of a lot of little holes in cardboard. It was essentially a mechanical operation.

Now observe the consequences of this and compare those consequences with similar consequences in other fields. It has been a commonplace throughout the ages that men famous for their race and lineage and inherited position were often surprisingly stupid. Why? Because when we hear that a man is eminent we naturally, though unreasonably, associate with the idea of his eminence something special to the man himself; such as courage, or brains. But there is no particular reason why an aristocrat should be more intelligent than a plebeian. The chance of finding a hero among a hundred lords is not a large one, anymore than it would be among a hundred peasants.

In the same way the eminence attaching to the mere possession of great wealth disappoints us nine times out of ten, especially if the wealth has been accumulated rapidly. For great wealth is accumulated rapidly by cunning or chance, or a mixture of the two. Cunning has nothing to do with high qualities; it is rather a presumption against them; while chance has nothing to do with them either. Therefore it is that men are always complaining after meeting So-and-so, that he seemed to be astonishingly stupid, though he made a million in ten years and started as a pauper. Most such men are stupid, compared with what we expect of them, but they are not stupider than the run of men; it is only the contrast between what they are and what we expected to find in them which makes us emphasize their very normal and average lack of parts.

So it is with the Scientist. Industry coupled with chance gives in his field of activity the reward of fame. Very great men indeed are to be found among the scientists, but it is not a scientific sense that has made them great; it is always some other talent. With Huxley, for instance, one of the very first of English names, mastery over the English tongue and an admirable intelligence were marks which would have singled him out in whatever activity he had undertaken. But side by side with him you have many another who has become equally or more famous through the mere accumulation of a mass of data by brute observation. Such plodding, carried on patiently and stupidly for the better part of a lifetime, may stumble on an important result—or may not. And for so stumbling on it no superior capacity is required. The same is true of scientific blundering or floundering into the apparent evidence for what turns out, later, to be false. Darwin's idea of the origin of species is an excellent example to the point. He accumulated a whole mountain of facts tending to establish development, or as it is now vaguely called, "evolution." In one department, that of human descent, what he had to say was very probably true*, but plenty of others had thought of it before him; in his only new contribution, his theory as to how evolution worked, he has proved to be simply wrong. Yet, so far as the fame of the market-place is concerned, Darwin is more famous than Huxley.

In general, the man who takes up the scientific method, whether in physics or history or in documentary criticism, takes it up with the more zeal because he knows that it is within the compass of the meanest intelligence. There is nothing to deter him. He can begin at once and work on those lines all his life, and myriads will be doing the same thing with equal pertinacity. The reward of fame being haphazard and having no quality about it, it follows that the scientific spirit tends to disregard quality.

And there is another consequence of all this. Since the most famous scientist need not have any intellectual claim to fame, the chances are that he will be an Ass like you and me. But, being famous, his opinion will be reverently sought on a host of matters where it is worthless and especially on the nature of the universe, of morals, of society, where he has no sort of standing; and here he will challenge, in his innocence, such giants as Suarez and Aquinas whom he has never read.

VI

The evil done by the Modern Scientific Spirit (I wish there were some shorter and simpler name for it) is due to its prestige.

---

*At the time the author wrote this book of essays (1931), the great bulk of evidence showing Evolution to be unfounded and without scientific basis had not yet been published. —*Editor*, 1992.

It exercises an authority over men through the awe and admiration in which they stand of it.

The causes of this prestige are plain enough. Modern science, that addition to human science which has been made since Christendom broke up—and especially since the definitely anti-Christian movement of the eighteenth century—has achieved many great things, some of them startling in their novelty, others in their scale, others in their satisfaction of a need; and all these three types of achievement which are sometimes coincident have produced a profound effect upon the modern mind. It is distantly parallel to the effect produced by the wonder-worker, coupled with the effect produced by the hero who slays dragons, with the addition of the effect produced by an enormity.

Thus the sudden appearance of flight, the equally sudden appearance of the talking machine, had a violent effect through novelty. Wireless has an effect through enormity; it is the scale of the thing that impresses—to be able to talk through space to the ends of the earth. And again, rapidity of locomotion satisfies what is, for many, something of a need, while universality of mechanical locomotion has satisfied for the modern man living in modern cities a very urgent need—which was to get out of them.

Sometimes all these three effects of modern science are coincident, and the new discovery not only satisfies a need, but is astonishing in scale and suddenly novel as well.

Those who can speak in the name of that which has done such things naturally have prestige, and if that prestige is mixed up with a false philosophy they naturally become the vehicles and promoters and propagators of that false philosophy.

That the harm done through false action upon the soul is greater than the advantage obtained through the new material good must be admitted by anyone who has the elementary sense to observe that we only feel happiness or unhappiness through the soul.

Thus, to transport the human body rapidly from one place to another cannot be good in itself; it is only a good insofar as it satisfies what may be called, in the largest sense, a spiritual need: that is, insofar as it fulfills the desire of a living soul. But if the same men who by research and accumulation of practice have made it possible thus to transport the body rapidly are by a false philosophy tending to make men's lives ugly, miserable, evil and untrue, then they will only transport unhappiness; and unhappiness transported quickly is not better but worse than happiness transported slowly.

And here there should be remarked the curious connection between the success of modern science in one set of purely material things and its almost invariable concomitant of failure in another set of things equally material. Nearly all that Modern Science does, not only fails to fulfill the promise of material happiness, but carries with it some quite definite material evil, quite apart from moral evil. For instance, rapid transport has brought about something like a permanent massacre. It is making us callous to an appalling tale of deaths by violence and horrible suffering in the infliction of such deaths. It puts at the command of men far below the average income a new material good; power of covering great distances and thereby enjoyment of changing scene. But it accompanies this power with a vibration and din which are abnormal and the ultimate physical effects of which must be disastrous. Modern Science reproduces the human voice mechanically and the sound of musical instruments, but in the reproduction there is always something incomplete and usually something metallic and offensive. It enables us to build on a greater scale more rapidly, and more strongly than before; but the new material seems doomed to produce horrors, and the newly enlarged scale to increase them.

Now, this combination of success and failure is not accidental, it is organic; it proceeds from a spirit which regards important things as unimportant. Had that spirit, for instance, understood the value of leisure and quietude, it would have developed its mechanism with those ends in view. It has not understood them. In the same way Modern Science has given us cheap and regular heat indoors during cold weather, but it is so particularly offensive a form of heat compared with that of the open hearth that those who can afford it are pathetically constrained to imitate the old, healthy fireplaces and their glow, even while submitting to the new inconvenience. But even if these material, corporal evils were not present, that spirit would still be an evil; for whatever is opposed to truth will be opposed to goodness and to beauty. That is why we have before us the effect today of such a spirit in the abominations of the latest architecture and the latest sculpture and the hideous applications of Science to war, and the destruction of comfort in the name of "Hygiene"—a typically "scientific" word for the common word Health. But perhaps it is as well to use another word than health, for hygiene has by this time come to connote something different indeed from health.

VII

The evil we have been here examining is of first rate importance. It attacks the whole field of man's life and it attacks with particular virulence those good things which are the very chief factors in man's life; those things whereby life was in the past made tolerable.

Notoriously and upon all sides the spirit of which I speak is attacking true doctrine, that is, the Catholic Church. If it continues in power unmodified that spirit will sooner or later wage open and direct war against true religion, as it has for so long waged covert and indirect war against it.

It further tends to cut us off from our past and from tradition; but societies cut off from their traditions and from their past wither.

It has begun to confuse and to atrophy the power of clear reasoning. It has long made deeper and deeper inroads into the sense of beauty, which it may at last destroy.

It is our business, then, to combat the Modern Scientific Spirit with all our might.

As a rule it is much easier to point out an evil, and even to analyze its nature, than to prevent it or to suggest a remedy for it. Happily in this case the remedy is obvious; it can be briefly stated and appreciated the moment it is set down. The evil spirit of which I speak is a *fashion.* It is no more than a fashion. It is a corporate mood, the strength of which depends upon the tyranny of fashion. Now the solvent of any bad fashion is ridicule.

Our weapon against the Modern Scientific Spirit is ridicule—persistent, active, untiring; and never was there an easier target for the exercise of that salutary spiritual activity.

The Modern Scientific Spirit is patently open to attack by laughter from a hundred points, both in its theory and in its practice, and above all in the pretensions of its priesthood, high and low. Its muddle-headedness lies open to the simplest analysis. Its self-contradictions can be tabulated by the score and are being added to daily. Its stupidity can be goaded, its pompous habit of baseless assertion exposed, its hideous creations in apparatus pilloried; there is not an aspect of it which does not lend itself to our shafts or which has any shield except obscurantism.

It has no defense against the attack of ridicule save continued and loud self-praise, reiteration, and perhaps (with the baser parts of society) clumsy appeals to lethargy.

Thus where it is riddled by the use of logic it can turn to its dupes and say, "Do not listen to this, it is only logic chopping. You would not bother with such a flimsy highbrow thing as logic, would you?" Or it can play the trick of confusing the issue, in which the master example is a confusion between Science proper and that which calls itself the Scientific Spirit.

With an appreciation of that form of defense I will conclude. It is the only serious obstacle to our advance against the silly but dangerous thing which pretends to speak in the name of true knowledge.

I have noticed that wherever the evils and perils of the Modern Scientific Spirit are attacked, those wounded in the attack and wincing from the pain of it raise, almost always, the cry that Science is being attacked; just as men who propose some foolish war in which the national finances may go under and which can be, even if victorious, of no profit, shriek that those opposing their policy are no patriots; just as a drunkard in his last stages still complains that those who would wean him from his mortal vice are the enemies of good-fellowship. I will bargain that of those few who have done me the honor of reading or skimming through this very long essay, some goodly proportion will lie open to this confusion of ideas and will need the warning that those who attack the perversions of Science are not attacking Science itself, but defending it.

There is not, and cannot be, any quarrel between sane reason and the search for truth. Our quarrel, and it is a serious one (I should say, in the long run, a *mortal* one), is with a moral atmosphere which, so far from making the discovery of truth its aim, is what I have called it: The Enemy of Truth. It is the Enemy of Truth because it is an enemy of the human reason and of the only methods whereby reality may be grasped.

The accusation that an attack upon these evils is an attack upon the immemorial human glory called Science must necessarily have some effect, and an effect widespread in proportion to the stupidity of those for whose benefit the accusation is made. Let that be no check to the efforts of those who have already begun, by ridicule, to break up the foundations of the maleficent structure. It is only a matter of pertinacity and time. Ill fashion always yields at last to the comic spirit, if that spirit be maintained. Laughter has already shaken those walls and, prolonged, will make them crumble.

THE SCHOOLS

The right of the parent over the child is prior to the right of the State. Where the State compels the parent to send its child to an institution which he must attend for many hours of the day and by which his mind cannot but be formed at the most critical period in its development, the parent has a right to demand of the State that the institution shall be of a kind he approves of. In the particular case of the Catholic parent living under the authority of an anti-Catholic state such as England, the members of the Catholic body have a full political right to claim that the whole expense incurred in the compulsory education of their children shall be defrayed by the State but shall be in Catholic hands—subject of course to the condition that money levied for a particular purpose must be spent on that purpose and that money levied for education must be spent on education. Whether it be possible in practice to obtain the whole of this rightful claim has nothing to do with its righteousness. We must always present the full claim and never compromise on it as a principle, whatever we may have to accept in practice. By steady insistence on the full and reasonable right, we can familiarize opponents with the idea of that right. The current and meaningless phrase, that "sums paid out of public funds must remain under public control" is as easy to expose as any other parrot-cry. The Catholic schools have a rightful claim to complete independence from the anti-Catholic state under which they exist. To talk of "neutrality" in this connection is silly or false, according to the character of the man who uses the word.

11

THE SCHOOLS

The education of the child belongs properly to the parent, and not to the State. The family is prior to the State in right, and this is particularly true of rights over children.

This is a very plain elementary Catholic doctrine on which there can be no discussion and no two views—though, as it must be with all doctrines, there can be any amount of discussion upon the application.

When the families of a State, or any great number of them, are too poor or demoralized, or for any other reason unable to bring up their children as useful members of the community, when they have been despoiled of their land, homes and property, as modern capitalism has despoiled them, when their succour by the spontaneous action of the rich is no longer in fashion, *then,* under such unnatural conditions, it may be the duty and sometimes *is* the duty, of the State to step in and help them. It is even conceivable that there might be circumstances in which it was the duty of the State to bring up certain children altogether. But, at any rate, the original right, as well as the original duty, is with the parents and not with the State. That is our doctrine, and it is one of the many in which we completely contradict the doctrine of the society in the midst of which we live, the which being contradicted, loses its temper.

Now, the society in the midst of which we have to live, being an anti-Catholic society, and propounding the opposite doctrine, to wit: that the State has the prior right over the child, not only contradicts our doctrine, but is—as inevitably follows sooner or later from such contradictions—at issue with us in a practical matter of daily life. It says, "I take your child as of right and educate him as I choose."

Here let it be remarked that this false doctrine, like all other false doctrines, lives "in the air," remote from reality. That is the very mark of false doctrine: that it has not roots in the soil: it cannot come down to earth. Men, in spite of themselves, instinctively recognize true doctrine, even when they are acting against it; and in this particular case of education the pompous people who, as parliamentarians and officials, claim the right to order us, recognize the prior right of the family by the very simple test that, even while they are making laws compelling other parents to give up their child to the conduct of the State, they would be horrified to find themselves under similar compulsion. *They* bring up their children according to their own views, and at the full discretion of themselves, the parents. This is because laws of this kind are made by the rich to be applied to the poor. There never was a time since Christendom began when the mass of men had less to do with the way in which they were governed; but this point of elementary education is a particularly glaring example. The first care of those who are most loud in proclaiming, not only the right of the State to educate the child, but the specific way wherein it shall be educated and the State doctrine in which it is to be brought up, are the most careful in their own lives to prevent anything of the kind happening to their own offspring. They select with great care those who are to guide their children for a part of the year. They hesitate long between this school and that, this tutor or governess and that; they make it of prime importance that the child shall have a particular kind of education which will make it like themselves in religion and culture. I should like to expose their humbug by making a drastic experiment peculiar to England, and show by a very practical example how vile the hypocrisy of State education in our case is. I should like to take half a dozen among the wealthiest of the chief doctrinaires in State compulsion and compel them to send their sons to schools where they should be taught to speak a fine Cockney accent and to call a napkin a serviette. It would clear their minds of cant and make them understand how and why false doctrine keeps out of touch with reality.

This mortal tyranny varies with various States. In the Catholic countries where an anti-Catholic—or rather anti-clerical—clique still holds the machine—the caucus of which is ironically called "Representative"—the grasp of the State is unrelenting. It appoints the teachers, forms their characters in anti-Catholic central institutions and everywhere affirms its right to decatholicize the children of the nation. Of these France presents the worst example, and it is probable that the new masters of Spain will, so long as they can keep their precarious power by leave of the army, attempt something of the same kind. In Belgium, where there is, so far, a balance between clerical and anti-clerical organization, the Catholic parent is given back some part of his tax money to bring up his children in the right way. In Holland and the Reich, where a conflict must be avoided between a large Catholic minority and a Protestant majority, two kinds of schools exist, each supported out of the taxes at the same rate, and the parent can choose between them. It is a bad system, for it drills official history and the secondary effects of Protestant culture into the children (for instance, in the Reich it breeds a whole generation to despise and hate the Catholic nations to the east and west, Poland and France), but at least it does not directly violate the right of the parent to have his child in a Catholic school. In Scandinavian countries, which are virtually homogeneous in religion and where Catholicism, a late arrival, was earliest stamped out, the problem does not arise. Nor does it arise in Italy, where the nation is homogeneously Catholic and where the anti-Catholic and Masonic organizations have been effectually got rid of by the happy suppression of Parliaments and all their sham authority, which is but a mask for a few rich men controlling a corrupt machine.

But in England there is a particular problem which specially concerns the greater part of my readers and which should also be of interest in other English-speaking countries where conditions differ from ours.

With that problem I propose to deal.

In the particular case of England, Catholic parents are compelled to send their children to be educated by the State unless they are rich enough to pay substantial sums for their private education; and the State is not only non-Catholic, but anti-Catholic.

We need not waste any time in the definition of the word State here; whether it calls itself a local authority or a central government, it is all one. The institution is a public institution, acting for public ends under the character and color of the State.

But the State in England has recognized in some degree, grudgingly and imperfectly, the justice of the Catholic claim to separate education, though it refused anything but a very limited degree of freedom. The State has, in England, reluctantly listened to (without accepting) the doctrine which itself denies; for it has allowed the parent to retain a certain very limited control over the education of his child. Where the difference in opinion between the parent and the State on what a child should be taught and in what surroundings it should live is strong enough to demand recognition the State has, to some extent, recognized the demand.

The motives of this recognition on its part are very mixed. It is partly that there has been at work the momentum of historical development. The English preparatory school system began as an institution founded on a voluntary school system and had to take over some of the characteristics of the voluntary system. Then there was the presence, peculiar to England, of the governing class of squires intimately connected with the official Church, which Church, not being that of the nation as a whole, and having started schools of its own, long insisted (it is now weakening) on recognition of private rights for itself and therefore rendered it difficult to deny such rights to others. Then there was the confused liberal notion that toleration was in some way a virtue in itself. The dread of being called intolerant if he compelled a child to learn a religion which was not that of its birth and baptism made the average nineteenth century English Parliamentarian uncomfortable. Then there was—a potent factor though carefully concealed—the secret sympathy of many highly cultured men among the bureaucrats, and of many from among the governing class at large, for the Catholic as against the anti-Catholic in this particular respect. Your well-educated Civil Servant would sometimes read and always believe anti-Catholic history. He would not admire Catholic culture. He would even probably know very little about it. But he disliked the moral system of a Puritan culture as something inferior to his own, and he had a soft place in his heart for a minority which was struggling to prevent its children being contaminated by that culture.

Whatever the mixture of motives was, the fact remained. The exception took root and has survived. The English Catholic schools exist, and have now the tradition of a lifetime behind them. A very great part of the total expense incurred in the compulsory education of Catholic children comes out of public money. What the proportion is exactly I do not think anyone has stated. Perhaps nobody *could* state it with close definition, because the calculation necessary to arrive at it would be a very complicated one. We have to reckon the money we have spent on putting up our schools, the sacrifice made by those who have taken lower salaries for the sake of keeping Catholic education alive, and a dozen other forms of expense, direct and indirect, less heavy now than in the past, but continuing today.

In this situation what we have before us as a practical political problem is this: To maintain the Catholic schools in England—I mean, of course, the Catholic schools under the compulsory system as applied to poorer people, for all this has nothing to do with the privileged rich—and, as an ideal, the full maintenance of our Schools out of public money.

Let us talk of the ideal first, because it is more important than the practical, since the practical is only the consequence of the ideal.

We have a moral right to the *complete* maintenance of our schools out of public money of which *we*—not the State—shall have the administration. We have the right to it on two grounds: first, that the State compels us to keep up such schools under the penalty of stepping in itself and weakening or destroying our children's religion. Secondly (and this is less important), because we ourselves pay rates and taxes into a common fund which is used for the most part to support anti-Catholic ideas.

Usually the second point is put first, and even made the only one; but if we analyze the matter clearly we shall see that, important as it is, it comes second in importance. Certainly the fact that we pay rates and taxes gives us a right to a proportionate amount of the money spent, but even if we were so poor that we could not pay rates and taxes, even if we were a small and completely pauperized community, unable to buy taxed tobacco or beer or coffee (this is an extreme supposition) and compelled to live in public barracks, where our rent did not include rates, we should still have a right to have our children educated in our religion rather than in another religion. Let that principle always be kept clearly in mind and well rubbed in, because it is an unfamiliar moral truth to the people around us. It is our duty, then, to aim at, and our right to attain, *full* provision. We have already got much the greater part of our current expenses paid out of public funds. We ought to aim at, and we have a right to attain, the ideal of having the *whole* of our expenses, current, building, permanent, paid out of public funds.

As against this right and duty, our opponents put forward two arguments, very strong in their own eyes. We can see their two arguments to be worthless; but it is our business in this struggle to understand why these arguments seem so strong to our opponents. We already know why they seem worthless in our own eyes, but you can never bring anyone to your point of view by merely condemning his. Our opponents object to our claim: (1) on the ground that elementary education need have no regard to the various sects into which they think the community is divided, and (2) that any sums paid out of public money should be subject to public control.

As to the first of these arguments, note carefully that our opponents sincerely believe English families to be divided into a great number of sects, one of which is as good as another (or as worthless as another), or, at any rate, all of which must be looked at indifferently by the State, since it cannot hope to reconcile them. Further, they argue, quite rightly, that the State cannot adjust itself to all the thousand and one differences between the Protestant sects; from Protestant pantheism, which is perhaps the largest, to Wesleyans and Baptists and Puseyites and Plymouth Brethren and Seventh Monarchy Men and Peculiar People—nor can I omit from the list a delightful sect peculiar to the little village of Loxwood, which mourns at a birth and rejoices at a burial.

They tell us that if the State is to succeed in what it is trying to do, to wit, instruct in elementary civic matters, it cannot burden itself and hopelessly complicate its task by special consideration for each and all of these numerous and various doctrinal systems. They also say, with truth, that an increasing number of families care nothing about doctrine; but they do not add that, though doctrine is forgotten, Protestant Ethics remain.

Now, here there are two very plain errors. In the first place, England is *not* divided into a great quantity of religious sects, like a sort of mosaic. Englishmen who are of Protestant tradition in culture—that is, the overwhelming majority of Englishmen, say nine tenths—were [formerly] divided, if you like, into a mosaic of sects, the marking lines between which have grown dim, and of which some have recently disappeared. Doctrines have faded into opinions, and with very many, probably the great majority, opinions have faded into indifference, where transcendental things are concerned; but the tradition and morals, the whole social stuff of the Protestant culture, remain. Between that culture and the Catholic there is a gulf. It is true, that even within the Protestant English culture there are not a few sympathizers with Catholicism; these are especially strong among the agnostics, and among a certain number of highly cultivated men in the English Church. But take the nation as a whole, and the line of cleavage is between a small Catholic body and the rest.

It is as though you were to take a man into a cellar where there was a vast collection of what we call temperance drinks, and what the Americans call soft drinks. In among them let there be a certain small proportion of bottles which held brandy. The soft drinks would differ among themselves very much in taste and color; some of them might even be discovered to contain a very small proportion of alcohol; but the real difference in the whole collection would lie between the brandy and all the rest. I think that all will admit this truth, whether they are of those who think brandy to be of the devil or of those who think it a great and good gift of God—especially if it be matured in the wood and come over from the Charente valley, or from the Campo Romano in Spain.

I remember some years ago a distinguished opponent of mine, who, in controversy with me upon this matter (he was a man whom all revered, for his age and honorable appearance, for the sincerity of his convictions, for his long white beard, and for his degree of Doctor of Divinity, which had been granted to him by a small college for blind negroes in the Southern States of America), would, in denouncing "Rome on the Rates," point out that he himself did not demand special grants of public money, though he had strong convictions on Adult Baptism which were not shared by the Congregationalists, for instance. What the outstanding truth which this opponent of mine had not perceived was, that between himself and a Congregationalist there was not enough difference to make education in common an anomaly or an injustice, let alone unworkable. If you were a Congregationalist rich enough to get private education for your son, you would not be horrified at the proposal to have a Baptist tutor for him; nor if you were a Baptist would you be horrified by the idea of a Congregationalist tutor, but you certainly *would* be startled in either case at a proposal that you should get a Catholic priest to come in and put the lad through his Latin.

The other error involved in this position is the idea that, since most of the things taught in the elementary schools have nothing to do with doctrine, therefore the doctrines held by those who teach cannot affect the children in an elementary school.

The error is so obvious that one wonders it has not been exploded long since, until one remembers that it is true of all errors that their mistake is obvious enough, when it is pointed out, and hardly ever perceived until it is pointed out.

This error consists in forgetting that association between

human beings, and particularly between a teacher and a child, is not mechanical but organic. If I am buying a book of the multiplication tables to give them to my child that he should learn them by heart (and I count no man as educated unless he knows the multiplication table up to 12 times 12 by heart, though I will let him off 11 times 13), I am quite indifferent whether the printer who set up those tables, or the publisher, was an active persecutor of the Church or a shining saint in the third order of St. Francis; and it makes no difference whatever to the child who learns the multiplication tables by heart what the doctrine of their printer or publisher was. But the moment you get outside this very narrow category of mechanical things, the moment the organic enters into anything, then doctrine, and the consequences of doctrine, come pouring in like a flood. The tone of voice of the teacher alone, it would not be extravagant to say the expression of his face, his gestures, certainly his allusions, his likes and dislikes, which the child discovers (directly or indirectly), and (much more important) his *reasons* for liking or disliking them—all that comes in.

Nor is this only true of the teacher; it is true of the thing taught. One of my fellow members in the House of Commons used to say to me: "After all, you cannot teach religion in arithmetic." To which I would answer, that in the first place you could teach religion in arithmetic, and in the second place arithmetic is not the only thing taught.

Even, I say, in teaching arithmetic the moral character of the teaching appears. For instance, if you give a child an example in subtraction by taking three apples from six apples, you may or may not be a teetotaller, but if you say three bottles of beer from six bottles of beer the child would not get a teetotal impression of life from you. Again, as to arithmetic not being the only subject taught to children: In almost every other subject religion quite obviously enters. In history the thing is too plain even to require illustration. History which makes Drake a national hero is anti-Catholic history; history which makes out the Jesuits under Cecil's regime to be national villains, is equally anti-Catholic history; and in general our official Whig history is anti-

Catholic history. Or take the case of geography. Quite a little while ago the Dutch Minister complained, quite legitimately, in the public Press, of a textbook in which the children of our elementary schools were taught that Holland was a completely Protestant country. The writer of the textbook answered in the simplicity of his heart: "What, then, did the great Motley write in vain?—Was not the Dutch rebellion against Spain the heroic act of Calvinists?" To which the answer was given: "No, it was the act of taxpayers resisting an intolerable tax; and not till the rebellion had proceeded far did a religious element enter into it." Further, there are in Holland, to every three Dutch Protestants, two Dutch Catholics. You cannot teach geography without either thus mis-stating a fact, if your doctrine is false, or showing emotion in favor of or against a religious culture, or without emphasizing some things rather than others, which emphasis will betray your religion.

For instance, do you make out the development of a country to be due to its climate rather than to its race; or to its race rather than its religion? Then you are distinctly on one side of the barricade as against those who rather emphasize the human element than the material, and the spiritual rather than the temporal. Palestine means for all of us a place on the map where the old Jewish civilization flourished and also where Jesus Christ was put to death and buried. But it makes all the difference whether you emphasize the one or the other of the two aspects. If you emphasize the one you are of one philosophy, or if you emphasize the other, you are of the other philosophy. In the one the Jews are the characteristic of Palestine; in the other the Holy Sepulchre.

The point of public control over public money has been misunderstood because people today will not think in terms of reason, but are led away by the jangle of words. The money paid away is "public," and therefore the control of it ought to be "public." It reminds me of the old story which Maupassant used to tell to his friends. He overheard a man saying: "For my part I am *logical*. If the house is mine I can turn my wife out of it." *Logical* was the operative word in this ineptitude, and "public" is the operative word of the ineptitude under consideration. Why on earth should the source of payment necessarily determine the control of it after it is made?

If I give ten shillings to a schoolboy out of the kindness of my heart, it is my ten shillings that I give. Have I therefore a right to control the way in which the lad spends it? When I pay my tailor, have I later on the right to object to his going on holiday with the money? When the State pays the Income Tax collector his wages, does it watch his movements and decide whether he shall wear brown boots or black? When I pay my Income Tax, have I a word to say on the way in which some specific part of it shall be spent? It is true that a man giving his money may nor may not give it on conditions. But to say that *because* the money is Jones's money, therefore, after it has been handed over, it must always be spent as Jones shall continue to dictate, is balderdash.

The State, in handing over money for a particular purpose—to wit: education—has a right to ask that it should be spent upon the purposes named. If it be a free gift, it has also the right to limit the application thereof. But here there is no question. It is not a free gift; it is a payment made as of right. It is a debt. The State says: "You must spend so much money on education, which you as taxpayers must supply." We answer: "Then we must receive that money which we have given you back from you for that purpose. We *will* spend it upon education—and you, the State, have a right to see that it is spent upon education and not upon sweetmeats or fireworks. But you cannot, merely because it proceeds from yourself, profess a natural right to make the expenditure of it conform exactly to what you yourself approve. No doubt you would like all education to be, as you call it, non-sectarian; that is, of the average well-defined English Protestant type which the great mass of citizens thoroughly approve. We happen to be a dissentient body to whom this Protestant character is as odious as we are to it. If you permit us to exist and to carry on our worship; if you call it immoral, as you do call it immoral, to prevent our doing so; if you say we have a right to continue our Catholic families, then you cannot insist upon your special religion, though it be that of the vast majority of the people, being imposed upon ourselves. The plea that because the money was paid to you and is received back by us, you have the right to say exactly how it is to be spent apart from its general intention, is valueless. Were that doctrine true, no Catholic school could exist under a non-Catholic government."

Of course, if you argue from the premise that the English polity is not anti-Catholic in character and that a state school will hence have no anti-Catholic effect on its pupils, and that therefore you are not persecuting our religion when you compel us to send our children to your schools, why then you are arguing from a falsehood and your deduction is worthless. It is as though you were to say: "There is no real difference between beer and other liquids," and on the strength of that falsehood compelled all the teetotallers to drink beer or die of thirst.

There stands one part, and one part only, of the claim to public money *under a compulsory system* for the support of our schools, such money to remain under our control as the only judges of what is and what is not a Catholic education. Of course, if there were neither tax-paying nor compulsion in the matter the claim would not lie. Even if there were a tax levied by the non-Catholic State for its own non-Catholic education, the claim would be modified. I have to pay for a host of State activities, any one of which I may dislike. But when the State says, "You *must* have your child taught," when it thus compels, it at once follows that to teach it things, or to teach it under conditions, which will endanger its religion is indefensible—save, indeed, on the plea that the religion is outlawed.

I have taken the English example because it is the one I know best; but the argument equally applies to all States where the modern fashion of State compulsion in education is at work.

The principle is vital. How far it must be waived in practice is another matter. A dead man's estate may owe me a sum larger than its whole amount; a robber who has stolen my goods may be undiscoverable; a swindler who has deprived me of my fortune may be too powerful with the politicians for me to recover

[it] in their courts of law. But in none of these cases does a man forgo his right in principle or fail to state it, though he is compelled in greater or less measure to yield. So it should be in the matter of the schools. We should state our full claim and never compromise on the full doctrine behind it. We should keep it alive and familiarize all our opponents with it, the more because it seems to them so strange. On this active presentation of the case depends the ultimate survival of our schools. And this is life and death in all countries to the Catholic community therein. For upon the schools depends the continuance of the Faith.

THE REVIVAL OF LATIN

There can never be peace in our civilization nor a common understanding until we have a common language. No artificial common language is worth considering. Latin—which is still the possession of a very large body of people; which was for all the time during which Europe was united and for long after the common language; which is easily learnt; which stands at the origin of all our culture—is the obvious medium.

12

THE REVIVAL OF LATIN

I wonder how far I shall carry any opinion with me when I plead for active effort to revive the general use of Latin?

It has always seemed to me one of those necessary reactions without which we shall be unable to reestablish the unity of Christendom. The longer we defer making the effort, the harder the effort will become; yet it is hardly more than 200 years since Latin was still the common medium of understanding on serious matters among Europeans, and not 300 years since it was the necessary medium for discussion on subjects common to all nations.

It was not replaced by French as a diplomatic language till after the middle of the seventeenth century. It was in general use in Eastern Europe, especially in Hungary, in Poland and the Lower Danube districts till much later. Even during the Great War one important international speech was made in Latin at the moment when the Bulgarians threw in their lot with the Prussian Reich under the certitude that it would come out victorious.

The problem presented is simply this: There is a common civilization, abominably warped by the religious revolution and ruin miscalled "The Reformation," but still in the main one thing. There is another name for this civilization. It used to be called Christendom; it is now sometimes vaguely called "the white races," or, more exactly, Europe. At any rate there is one unmistakable thing which, in spite of a badly diseased and divided social state, is still in the main the common descendant of the old Christian culture. Its dress, its manner of living, its main social ideas are the same.

Inter-communication between its various parts is absurdly interrupted by profound differences of idiom. The different national languages are thus separated precisely because there used to be a common medium, and because it was therefore thought no menace to unity that the vernacular languages should flourish. Latin was the common language and the bond between all men of European stock.

The necessity of some common language is seen in the fantastic attempts to create one artificially. You will find enthusiasts for stuff like Esperanto, which is about as much like a human language as a jigsaw puzzle is like a living face. Such enthusiasts seem never so much as to have heard that Latin was for century after century the common living tongue of our race. It enshrined half the greatest of our literature, nearly all our traditions, all our religion—yet no one has a word to say for it now as an international medium!

There was a moment when it looked as though French would take the place of Latin, at any rate with cultivated people; but the growth of an exasperated nationalism, the vast expansion of the New World, and the victories of Prussia during the nineteenth century wars have made that impossible. It would have been better than the chaos in which we now live, but a poor substitute for Latin save in this, that French is a living language.

It is, by the way, just as well for the French that the thing did not happen, because nothing is worse for a local language, or for the nation that speaks it, than to be internationalized. We are already seeing the pathetic effects of this on our own nation and speech; the decay of English, its rapid vulgarization and weakening, are due to its sprawling undisciplined over such incongruous lands.

Outside the training of men for the Catholic priesthood, and one or two special areas such as Scotland, Latin gradually became in the West of Europe, after the Reformation, the privilege of the wealthier classes. Today it is not even that. But the fact that it was once so has, I believe, done a great deal to prejudice people against it. The prejudice has some foundation in reason; for if Latin were indeed to be the test of an expensive education, then, since only a small and wealthy class could afford to know it, the mass of men would have good right to protest against its use, for by such a custom they would be cut off from public discussion.

There has further grown up in connection with the use of Latin an idea—false, but also natural—that there was something specially difficult about that tongue. On the contrary, it is the easiest of all foreign languages to learn because it is the most clear and logical, and because so many of our words in all languages are connected with it.

Of all subjects which our modern and dangerous machine for compulsory instruction insists upon putting into the young, Latin is the one of which they talk least and the one of which they wish to know least. That Latin is more necessary to the plain man than reading the vernacular I won't say, and I think it is not more necessary than to be able to keep very simple accounts. But it is a great deal more necessary than unproved theories on health, or than "nature study," or than the already false and warped national history that is put before the young, officially, in the official schools. It is even more necessary than elementary geography, and its general use would make all the difference in the relations between men of different countries.

Today the several Christian nations are quite cut off. There is only one international language, the Judaeo-Deutsch, called in English Yiddish; and that is only of service to a comparatively small segregated section of people, and is used more or less secretly. A Jew brought up to that use in say, Poland, will have a common medium wherewith to talk to his brothers in London, Paris or New York—and he uses it. But the Pole who comes to London, Paris or New York has no common medium wherewith to talk to his fellows of the Christian world.

There is only one obstacle to the revival of Latin, and this is, that the idea of it has been allowed to fall out. We are as unused to it today as our immediate forefathers were used to it. We take its absence for granted as they took its presence for granted; and I am persuaded that its revival would be the best merely scholastic reform we could undertake for reuniting our imperilled civilization.

In order to effect so salutary a change, how should we proceed? We have to hand most powerful instruments: all that is needed is the spirit that shall set them going.

We have for a nucleus the vast body of the Catholic priesthood, drawn from every rank in society and everywhere strongly grounded in Latin, using it daily in the liturgy and constantly in touch with its phrases and textbooks. All these hundreds of thousands are ready as a foundation for the general resurrection of Latin.

The modern usurpation of teaching by the State, amid all the evils it has bred, promises to permit one very good thing: which is the revival of that ancient Catholic idea, the presentation of superior education to all children whose parents care to give it them. When the Faith was universal any likely child who showed aptitude for scholarship could obtain it. Poverty was no bar. As a matter of common principle education was endowed, and all over Europe, even here in England before the wholesale robberies under Henry VIII, Edward VI and Elizabeth, one of the duties and functions of the well-to-do was to endow secondary schools, and in these the acquirement of Latin was the chief activity, so that there should be everywhere a large body who could use the common language of Christendom.

Today that idea of easy popular access to higher education is reappearing. It is reappearing in a cramped, base, mechanical form, with none of the old diversity and local feeling, but it is there and *might* be used to a good purpose. All are familiar with the conception that superior education should be open to those who desire it.

Provided the State does not lay its deadening hand upon the new development, nor exercise that blind tyranny of which it is today more enamored than was any despot in the past (and how tamely we submit!), the situation may be saved.

Even if the State so mars and deflects the new movement, and compels the mass of children who would have higher instruction to follow its cast-iron rules and learn only what it provides, *we* can in part escape. In those countries where some fraction of the taxes Catholics pay is allowed them for their own schools, they can give their new secondary schools, if they are careful to preserve them, a system of their own: and in that system they can restore the place and the prestige of Latin. If the practicing Catholic body in any country, even in one where Catholics are few, were known to be generally conversant with elementary Latin it would leaven the rest.

To do so would be part of that task which, in temporal things, is our main function—the true political vocation of the Catholic—to arrest, if it still be possible, the decline of civilization, to revive culture, to form of the Catholic body an army of leaders in the preservation and possibly the extension of our old glories now so grievously imperilled. *We* are the true heirs and guardians of civilization in the modern race to barbarism, and to reverse the current should be our privilege as well as our duty. The achievement is arduous, but possible. It should be our glory to obtain it.

An Article of Mr. Haldane's

A biologist of high distinction, by implication or by affirmation, touches upon those points where the Catholic Faith is at issue with the great bulk of men of his profession. The nature of this issue should be examined and the validity of the affirmations or implications tested, for work from such a pen is a good and typical instance of the conflict between Catholicism and the agnostic "scientific" world.

13

AN ARTICLE OF MR. HALDANE'S

In my daily paper of the morning on which I write these words I read an article of some length which is by far the most interesting thing in the sheet. It proceeds from the pen of Mr. Haldane, the deservedly distinguished biologist who stands in the very front rank of the generation junior to my own. It is because Mr. Haldane holds such a position, but also because his name stands for such a great tradition in England, that I have taken what he has written for the text of what follows. It is amusing, and sometimes profitable, to consider or to refute one of the host who are unequipped for dealing with the great theological problems, and who yet fill our time with silly repetitions of errors which have been exposed during hundreds of years. Their adventures in the obvious, their simple pride in discovering as novelties what men have discussed for thirty centuries are the absurdity of our time. There is quite a different interest in reading and considering the work of a man so really eminent as Mr. Haldane. His father, amid a mass of public work of the highest value, produced that essay on Vitalism (not yet, I hope, forgotten) which helped to change the thought of our time. His uncle was a statesman of the first rank, and more than any other man made possible the strength of England by land in the Great War. He was also among the greatest of English lawyers. Mr. Haldane's sister has an increasing name in literature, and his own achievement is one which every man of intelligence respects and admires.

It is on account of all this that I take a particular interest in dealing with certain points in Mr. Haldane's article which, by implication, challenge the Catholic position, and which also present at their best the attitude opposed to ours in modern intellectual life.

I do not propose to deal with the article as a whole, because it does not as a whole challenge conclusions of the Faith. It is concerned with modern life in general, and only in three significant passages touches upon that point of vital interest to myself (and I think to the writer), the quarrel between the best intelligences within the two camps; the camp of the Faith, the camp of those opposed to it. To consider work from such a pen is of real value, for, indeed, there is no equality of armament or method between the Catholic and any other opponent of his save the high skeptic. Our other opponents are lesser people with whom it is a pastime to deal, but the high skeptics are serious antagonists. For there are today but two essential attitudes possible: the skeptical and the Catholic.

The points I select as being of special interest to me in Professor Haldane's article are these:

First. The writer speaks of a fellow Catholic and literary colleague of mine, Mr. J. B. Morton ("Beachcomber," of the *Daily Express*) as being one of those fighting "a rear-guard action against the advance of science." It is a phrase which may be extended to the whole frame of mind which it implies. It is a phrase implying the statement that those who are of the Faith are falling back reluctantly from position to position, retreating before the triumphant and inevitable advance of something which can but destroy the Faith and which is labelled "Science."

Second. The writer, in what is perhaps the most interesting of all the sentences of this interesting article, expresses his intellectual preoccupation with a certain problem—which he puts thus, "Why millions of men have been persuaded that there is spiritual advantage in bathing in the water of the Ganges, or in believing in the doctrine of the Immaculate Conception." Mr. Haldane is quite rightly moved by the chief question facing mankind. It has been put in a very concise and striking form in the Gospels, "Is religion from God or from man?"

Third. Mr. Haldane in this very passage, using the phrase "Immaculate Conception," uses it for the doctrine known to Catholics as the Incarnation of God as man and His birth from a pure Virgin. I hope I am not misrepresenting him. I think I am rightly interpreting his intention, for as was the case with Mr. Wells and almost every other modern English writer on these affairs, that technical term of Catholic theology, "The Immaculate Conception," is thought to be identical with the term "Nativity"; that is, the doctrine that Jesus Christ, who was very God, was incarnate as man by divine generation through the Virgin Mary.

Now let us consider those three points in their order.

First of all, what about the "rear-guard action" against science?

Long before Brunetière (I think) launched that famous epigram, "The bankruptcy of science," a lifetime ago, the idea implied in the epigram has spread widely. During all our time there has been a latent and often open war between those who defend the Faith and those who tell us that they base themselves upon the impregnable conclusions of physical science: that is, the body of acquired demonstrable knowledge, tested by experiment, and not to be denied by the human reason.

On the nature of this quarrel I have written elsewhere in this book. What I am concerned with here is the operative word "rear-guard."

There is no doubt that those who defend the Faith are fighting with more and more vigor, and in increasing numbers, and with a rapidly accumulating wealth of illustration and argument the old academic position of the nineteenth century, which in a dozen ways believed itself to have triumphed over Catholicism (or, as they preferred to call it, the more guarded of them, "Dogma," the more sincere, "Christianity"). But the word "Catholicism" is the accurate word in this regard, for there is no meaning in "Christianity" unless it imply at least some fragment or distortion of the Catholic scheme. Of the intellectual vigor displayed by Catholicism today, I say, there is no doubt at all, even in England; in the larger air of Europe it is a commonplace. To deny the new activity of Catholicism as compared with its old timidity would be as foolish as to deny the change in men's attitude towards Parliaments, or towards the conceptions of "Progress," or any other sign of the awakening from ideas which were taken for granted a generation ago.

But is this activity the fighting of a rear-guard action? Is the Catholic effort losing ground?

I should have said that a general conspectus of Europe would lead to the exactly contrary conclusion. I am not here concerned with the truth or falsehood of the opposing philosophies. I am concerned with the question: "Which of the two sides, Catholic and Anti-Catholic, is occupying new ground? Which of them is giving way before the other?" A completely indifferent and detached mind, surveying Europe as a whole, can only conclude that the Catholic side is advancing. It may be regrettable. The Catholic advance may be, as Mivart said in old age, one more reaction of unintelligence against intelligence, comparable to the swamping of Buddhism by Brahmanism in the East. It may be the deplorable accompaniment of a decline in civilization comparable to the decline in art and letters at the end of the Roman Empire. It may be but one aspect of that deplorable fatigue which ruins high civilizations at their highest achievement—but *there it is*.

You may see it in any one of a dozen fields. Let me return to two I have touched on elsewhere. Half a lifetime ago everyone took it for granted that "scientific" criticism had destroyed the authenticity of the Fourth Gospel. It was not the testimony of an eyewitness. It was not due to St. John's experience of Jesus Christ. It was put together long after the date when the last of the contemporaries of Christ must have been dead. The traditional author, John the son of Zebedee, thus dethroned, could not have been the Beloved Disciple—and so forth. Where is all that mass of hypothesis and guesswork today? I do not say that it is disproved because fashion has changed. I do not here make fashion a criterion of truth. All I am saying is that fashion on this point *has* changed. The rejection of the Fourth Gospel "dates." The arguments used to destroy its value belong to the age of hansom cabs. Where in this matter is there a sign of "rear-guard action"?

You must not use the words "a rear-guard action" as the description of men who continually advance. Their advance may be a tragic example of intellectual decline in our civilization, just as the German breaking of the Allied line at St. Quentin in 1918 was tragic in our eyes. To us it was the deplorable success of what was worse against what was better. But not the wildest of patriots could have described the German advance upon Amiens during that Easter week as "a rear-guard action."

Take a parallel example in the field of what was called "Scientific" Criticism. What about the attitude on St. Luke's authorship of the Acts of the Apostles? Harnack, in famous pages, destroyed that criticism.

There was nothing Catholic about him. I do not think it unjust to a famous name to say that he did not understand what the Catholic Church was, nor, for that matter, is it Catholic doctrine to my knowledge that St. Luke wrote the Acts. It is certainly tradition, and may be common sense; it is not dogma, so far as I know. But no one can say that Harnack was "fighting a rear-guard action," still less that those of us, great Catholic scholars, or ignorant Catholic laymen like myself, are now taking part in a rear-guard action when we defend the claims of tradition. We were heavily pressed when Plancus was Consul, but today the pressure is the other way round. I say again, this change does not prove that we are right. The wrong side may be advancing and the right side retreating; but there is no doubt as to the direction of movement.

Or take Dom Chapman's "Studies in the Early Papacy"; is that a "rear-guard action"? It reads much more like a bombardment before attack.

Take another department in this same type of criticism, where Andrew Lang and others fought, in the old days, what was *then* called a rear-guard action: the nature of the Iliad and the Odyssey. Within living memory it was difficult to maintain that those two bodies of verse were the work of an individual poet. They were tribal songs strung together. They were nature myths. They were anonymous barbaric rhapsodies. Even if there had been a conscious recension of the one, it was not from the same hand as the conscious recension of the other. The Iliad and the Odyssey were every conceivable thing in turn, *except* poems by a poet; and those who knew what poetry was, having written it themselves, or having a sane taste on the subject, were thought to be out of court. There never was any Homer, and the Iliad and the Odyssey, arising popularly in a primitive society, grew up in any way you will, but not from the creative inspiration of one poetic genius.

Where are all those theories now? They are still held by many. I should be rash indeed were I in my ignorance to challenge those who still hold them; but it would be silly to pretend that the intellectual fashion in this matter has not changed. Can anyone say that Bérard is fighting "a rear-guard action"?

At this point I may be told that my examples are beside the mark. The traditionalist is not identical with the Catholic, nor are the methods of the old criticism, even when they are applied to the Canon of Scripture, necessarily an attack upon the Faith. All this is true; but the examples I have given illustrate the spirits of two camps in opposition. The Catholic temper is Traditionalist. Individual Catholics may indulge in almost any modern or belated vagary, so long as it does not contradict defined doctrine or specific moral commandment. But the Catholic temper as a whole reacts against that other temper which produced the old-fashioned methods once called scientific criticism, now so heavily discounted. It opposes them because it feels them to be at issue with reason. But whether it be right or wrong in opposing them, no one may doubt that such opposition has been going forward all through our time, and the other side going back.

Take another department where actual doctrine is concerned; the main body of non-Catholic learning in the past generation denied the will; we affirm the will. The great body of non-Catholic physical scientists was fatalist. Well, in this department also it is the reaction which has been winning. The old-fashioned materialistic Monism which was so widely spread half a lifetime ago is today nearly dead. The few people who still maintain it are surviving veterans, revered as antiquities. Indeed, the opposite tendency is actually exaggerated, and men are beginning to accept on far too slender evidence all manner of stories, supernatural or quasi-supernatural; anyhow, it is not the old materialism which has been winning, or the old fatalism either. The world is full today of voices, those of deluded men, of quacks, and of imperfect philosophers who give the will inordinate power; while others, more sincere, are proudly announcing it as a new discovery—absolutely modern—that if you resolutely direct your thoughts in the right direction you will improve your character. Only the other day I read two columns of this from the pen of a popular novelist in the very same paper which contained Mr. Haldane's article. The popular novelist not only thought himself ultra modern, but said so emphatically and over and over again. His attitude was: "Oh, that people would only appreciate the great results of recent research! Then they would learn the startling truth that we can improve ourselves by thinking about the right things and harm ourselves by thinking about the wrong ones." It certainly does not look as though in this department—will versus mechanics—Catholic doctrine were fighting a rear-guard action. I should say that it was rather time for us Catholics to put the brakes on, and check the spiritualists and faith-healers.

Now let me turn to the second point of those I have selected as typical of this piece of writing. Mr. Haldane professes his interest in that social phenomenon, the acceptation by millions of men of doctrines not based upon, and (in his view) contradictory to, demonstrable experience. He professes an eager interest in finding out how and why men fall under what its opponents call the religious illusion.

Now, Mr. Haldane's interest in this is an excellent proof of his high intelligence. One of the main marks of stupidity is the impatient rejection of mystery; one of the first marks of good judgment, combined with good reasoning power, is the appetite for examining mystery.

Mr. Haldane takes for his examples the belief of masses of orientals that bathing in the waters of the Ganges is of an effect beneficial to the soul of man, and the belief in the Incarnation—the belief that a Galilean who lived and died nearly two thousand years ago was, not only the man he certainly was, but also, born of a miraculous birth, the Omnipotent and Infinite God who made the universe. He wants to know "How men persuade themselves of such things?"—the implication being that all such ideas must be illusions.

Well, let us begin by thinking clearly in the matter; clear thinking is always of advantage when one is attempting to discover the nature of things.

There are here two distinct categories of implied affirmation. The first implied affirmation is that a relation between a seen, visible, natural world wherein truths are demonstrable by repeated physical experiment, and an unseen, immaterial, spiritual world (if any such exist) cannot be a real relation and can only be an imaginary one. Supposing there were a man in Galilee, presenting all the characteristics which we know from experience to inhere to the known object—a man; then it can but be an illusion to predicate of that man other characteristics which are not known by the senses or demonstrable by experience. And the greater the undemonstrable, unexperienced, unseen characteristics you predicate, the less credible your predication.

On the sanctity of the Ganges a parallel affirmation is implied. There is a tract of country over which flows a stream of water, and to this stream, though itself has no real unity, the mind of man gives unity and calls it by a name—the Ganges. The water has certain qualities demonstrable by experience. We all know what water is physically and what it will do and what it will not do physically. We can test by experiment what this particular water may be in its physical composition. To predicate over and above these known physical characters of a particular stream of water a number of unseen, immaterial spiritual attributes, is to nourish an illusion.

There you have the first affirmation implied in the statement I am examining. It is all of a piece with the general affirmation which denies the validity of a sacramental system, of shrines, in general of spiritual influence acting in, or being connected with, natural things.

The second implied affirmation is, that as this sort of illusion seems to crop up at random and to fix upon all manner of disconnected objects, it must proceed from the self-deceiving mind and corresponds to no external reality. In this specific instance you have myriads accepting the sanctity of the Ganges water, and other myriads accepting the divinity and miraculous generation of a particular, limited historical human being. The one is worth as much as the other and both are worthless.

Now let us examine these two affirmations. The first, the denial that there can be a connection between a spiritual world (if it exists) and a natural one is gratuitous; it relies upon no law of thought; still less upon any piece of experimental knowledge.

If you say: "This medal has the virtue of protecting men from bullets in a battle. So long as a man wears it he cannot be hit," that proposition can be subjected to experiment. You can distribute such medals to every soldier in a brigade going into action; you can see to it under the severe discipline of modern armies that the men actually wear the medals; and you can then see whether the singular unseen powers ascribed to the medals are real or not. But if it is affirmed that the medal has an influence of holiness, has an unseen effect upon the unseen and spiritual part of man (supposing there be anything immaterial), then you can believe or disbelieve the statement, but you cannot disprove it. To affirm that there can be no sacramental connection between the physical and the spiritual, that therefore the worship paid to every shrine, to every god inhabiting every grove, is an example of illusion, is an affirmation and nothing more.

If you say the thing is an illusion because it is not subject to some sort of test that would apply to physical processes, your affirmation is not only gratuitous, but against reason; for you are applying to one category what is proper to another. It is as though I were to say that Velasquez was not a good painter because no chemical analysis of the pigments used by him proved a sense of beauty in him.

The second affirmation, the affirmation that all such things are illusions because they are so separate, sometimes so contradictory, so numerous and sometimes so demonstrably false (as in the case of the medal that is said to be a charm against being killed in battle), relies upon false reasoning.

A good grasp of the logical principles involved should show this clearly. Because of ten similar conceptions nine are proved false, it does not follow that the tenth is false. For instance a man hears that there are ten very different pictures each said to be the portrait of his dead father, whom he remembers well. He travels about to inspect each in its place, and says of nine, one after the other: "That is not my father." He may then get weary of the process and say: "All these rumors are erroneous": but if he gives up the search on that account he is acting from emotion and not from reason; he is urged by fatigue or disgust, and not by the process of intelligence. For it may well be that the tenth, which he has not examined, will turn out to be indeed the portrait of his father which he was seeking.

Another way of putting it is the reply to the very true and forcible sentence: "Man is the only animal who makes gods." In that sentence most who use it mean to imply further: "And as one can show that many of these gods are man-made only; therefore, every God is man-made." But the true reply is: "This 'therefore' is unwarrantable. It may be that men make gods precisely because the instinct of worship is an instinct corresponding to a reality. And even though it were demonstrable (which it is not) that none of these twenty or a hundred gods you mention were real, but each and all of them figments of the imagination, it does not follow that some one other God may not be real—may not be that which the soul was seeking."

It seems to me of the first importance that this plain piece of reasoning should be correctly stated, followed and repeated whenever the controversy arises.

Let us take the particular example here given. The implication was: "We are all agreed that the water of the Ganges has no spiritual effect, and we may therefore be all agreed that the doctrine of the Virgin Birth is false." But in the first place, who knows whether the waters of the Ganges have or have not any spiritual effect? By what right do you affirm that it has none? If there are spirits, if there be a spiritual world, why may not a spiritual influence, good or evil, or neither good nor evil, be found working through a physical means or interconnected with a material object? You cannot prove by your reason that the thing is *not* so. You can *feel* that it is not so. You may be led by your *emotions* to sneer at the conception; but do not mistake your emotions for your reason. If it comes to mere emotions, my emotions are the other way about. I incline to the sanctity of shrines and to the presence of the unseen in groves and fountains, *More majorum,* as all our fathers did, Pagan and Catholic. You don't feel any such thing? That proves nothing. My emotions do not disprove yours, but then, your emotions do not disprove mine. That the thing is logically possible, granted the two worlds spiritual and physical, cannot be denied.

To sum up; it is our business, I think, to clear the ground in this great debate and to make our modern opponents comprehend what our position is—and how they are but affirming a faith contrary to ours when they think they are disproving it by a process which they take to be the use of the reason, but which, on analysis, proves to be the very negation of the use of the reason.

Now let me conclude with the third point I have chosen—the use of the term "Immaculate Conception" to mean "Incarnation through a miraculous birth."

It may seem a point too insignificant to be taken. After all (I may be told), it is but an error on a technicality. No one outside the secluded little world of Catholic theologians uses their technical terms or can give you the exact definitions of such terms. The swarm of modern English writers who are perpetually using the term "Immaculate Conception," wrongly imagining it to mean "Incarnation through a Virgin," are guilty only of a little slip in a quite unessential and excentric department of the discussion. The writers who have misused the terms have only to correct their proofs and write "Virgin Birth" where, by a piece of very natural ignorance, they had written "Immaculate

Conception," and all will be well. It is (I may be told) as though a Catholic defending the authenticity of the Johnnine comma (which by the way has not been defined as authentic) were to spell it "coma" instead of "comma." It would show him ignorant of Greek spelling, but Greek spelling is not the essence of the affair.

But wait a moment. The term "Immaculate Conception" means all this: "That the race of man suffers from an hereditary taint, proceeding from some action at its origin in which the will of man rebelled against the will of God, and this original taint is called Original Sin. But of the human race" (says the Catholic definition promulgated in the nineteenth century) "there is one exception to this rule, to wit, the Mother of Jesus Christ." *That* is the doctrine of the Immaculate Conception.

The doctrine of the Incarnation is something quite different; it is the doctrine that Jesus Christ was not only man, but also the Infinite God incarnate in that Man and was born of a divine and miraculous Maternity. To confuse the two doctrines is like confusing the atomic hypothesis with the series of atomic weights, or the term "vitalism" with the term "vital statistics."

It is, then, a startling error in a point of fact. And is it so unimportant after all—an error of this kind? Does it not rather betray the fact that even the most eminent men in the camp opposed to us, and even those most readily prepared to consider this strange phenomenon called religion, do not know what men of average education ought to know? Does not so widespread an error as this, though it only concerns two technical terms in the particular department of theology, argue that our opponents have lost, in some degree, their sense of historical proportion and, in that degree, their power of appreciating truth?

The doctrine of Original Sin has been of the first consequence to the world. It has vitally affected the formation of all our culture. It largely explains the political history of Europe since Europe first became Christian. The worship of our Blessed Lady also, and its culmination in the doctrine of the Immaculate Conception, has been of immeasurable effect upon that culture. However thoroughly one may be convinced that both these things are nonsense, one cannot pass them by as immaterial, as being something on which there is no need to have even general knowledge; for no European can know the past of his race, nor understand how he came to be what he is, who has not some general conception of that Religion which formed us.

When Monsieur Briand alluded a short time ago to the Council of Trent as "The Council of Thirty Men," the slip was rightly pointed out by his opponents as a proof that he was not competent to deal with European diplomacy. The word "Trente" in French means both the town of Trent and the number thirty; but the man who knew so little of the formation of Europe as not to know that there had been a Council held at Trent certainly could not understand from what roots the present international complications spring. He was like a man who should be discussing modern English politics and attempting a solution of our industrial troubles under the impression that the word "statute" meant "statue"—and anyone making that mistake in his efforts at the reconciliation of capitalist and proletarian would not be taken seriously.

I do not sneer at those who (in this country and America alone, I think) fall into the elementary error of mistaking the Immaculate Conception for the Miraculous Birth, anymore than I should sneer at a distinguished Chinaman, who, not having traveled in Europe, thought (like a recent Prime Minister of England) that the Dalmatian coast was on the Baltic, or, like another Cabinet Minister, that the Dardanelles were at the Gibraltar end of the Mediterranean. The Chinaman might be a very great figure in his own country and might reply with justice that the particular position of the Dalmatian coast left him cold. But I do say that to discuss Catholic ideas and in doing so to mix up the Immaculate Conception with the Incarnation through a miraculous birth is to show oneself unacquainted with the subject one is criticizing. It is an error which the more often it is made, the better proves that our opponents have not yet learnt the alphabet of that which they think they are about to destroy.

THE FAITH AND INDUSTRIAL CAPITALISM

Industrial Capitalism is a manifest evil. It cries out against our sense of justice, its products offend our sense of beauty, the society based on it is not only vile but increasingly unstable. It came into existence through Calvinism, which was the vital principle informing all the revolt against the Faith at the origin of modern times. Yet there is no specific principle in Industrial Capitalism which can be doctrinally condemned. No Catholic can deny the rights of property, or of free contract. No Catholic can join the efforts made to be rid of the evils of Industrial Capitalism by way of civil war or tyranny. Least of all can any Catholic have anything to do with the inhuman system called "Communism." The remedy for the evils of Industrial Capitalism will not be found in any Socialistic action or theory developed under the very same false philosophy as produced Industrial Capitalism. We know that the remedy would be worse than the disease. The disease will never be remedied until the mind of society has been changed by conversion to the Faith.

14

THE FAITH AND INDUSTRIAL CAPITALISM

If there is one mark more striking than another about the Catholic Church it is its intellectual freedom.

The moment a Catholic goes outside and lives with people not under the influence of the Church he finds himself in an atmosphere of intellectual convention which to a man of Catholic habit is stifling. Perhaps I ought to call it "intellectual faith" rather than "intellectual convention," for the simplicity and tenacity with which intellectual doctrines are taken for granted outside the Catholic Church much more resembles the simpler and more childlike forms of faith than a social convention.

People outside the Catholic atmosphere seem to take as a matter of course the intellectual fashion of their time; and never, within my experience, at least, go to first principles and ask themselves why they accept that fashion. One comes across this tiresome petrifying of the intellect in all directions. In the acceptation of majorities, for example; in the swallowing whole of official history; in the blind acquiescence in the right of the State to take control of education; in the bland repetition of newspaper science and newspaper politics. An excellent instance is the attitude towards miracle. Mention an historical miracle, and the man unfamiliar with Catholic truth denies it at once: without consideration of the evidence. But when you are discussing with Catholics an historical event in which the marvelous *may* have entered you get free discussion, one man saying he believes in the miracle and giving his reasons, another saying he does not and giving *his* reasons; while for the most part those who take one side or the other at least imply their first principles and often state them.

It is all part of the process which others than Catholics are beginning to realize, that, outside the Faith, men are abandoning reason.

Now one of the consequences of this intellectual freedom produced in the mind by the influence of the Faith is that Catholics may and do hold an infinity of positions upon matters where the general trend of Catholicism is manifest, but where there has been as yet no theological definition, or where in the nature of things there can be none.

The most important of these in temporal matters today is the attitude of the Catholic towards Industrial Capitalism.

There is and can be no doctrinal decision either for or against the morality of Industrial Capitalism. On the other hand, no one will doubt that Catholicism is in spirit opposed to Industrial Capitalism; the Faith would never have produced Huddersfield or Pittsburg. It is demonstrable that historically, Industrial Capitalism arose out of the denial of Catholic morals at the Reformation. It has been very well said by one of the principal enemies of the Church, and said boastfully, that Industrial Capitalism is the "robust child" of the Reformation and that the vitality of the effect proves the enduring strength of the cause. It is equally clear that the more Catholic a country is, the less easily does it accommodate itself to the social arrangement of a proletariat subjected to millionaire monopolists.

Yet not only is there no doctrine which can be quoted to contradict any one of the necessary parts of Industrial Capitalism, but there are a sufficient number of excellent Catholics who will actively defend it.

No one can say that it stands condemned specifically by Catholic definition, for what is there in Catholic morals to prevent my owning a machine and stores of livelihood? What is there to prevent my offering these stores of livelihood to destitute men on condition they work my machine, and what is there in Catholic morals to forbid my taking a profit upon what they produce, receiving from such production more than I lay out in the sustenance of the laborers? And as for individual Catholics supporting Industrial Capitalism, nine well-to-do Catholics out of ten do so in practice by the way they live and by the way they make their investments, while at least one wealthy Catholic out of ten (I should guess a much larger proportion) is ready to defend Industrial Capitalism and even to grow eloquent about it, rightly contrasting it with the evils of anarchy or insufficient production, or the menacing tyranny of Communism.

What is even more significant—when, in a nation of Catholic culture such as France or Italy, Industrial Capitalism takes root, then the fiercest revolt against it on the part of the poor does not spring from the more Catholic workmen, but from the less Catholic. The masses of a Catholic proletariat—where such masses exist—are upon the whole docile to Industrial Capitalism. They are not in such active revolt against it as their anti-Catholic fellows. Upon the Continent they actually form Trade Unions proud to call themselves Catholic and specially distinguished by their refusal to admit class conflict between employer and employee. Moreover, take the modern world at large and you will see that on whatever portions of a Catholic country Industrial Capitalism has laid its hands, the capitalist class and the system which it maintains defends the Catholic Church as a bulwark of its power, and conversely that in those places (Barcelona, for instance) the Catholic Church is particularly attacked by those who wish to destroy Industrial Capitalism.

So far, so good. We all admit that in theory there is no precise logical definable conflict between Industrial Capitalism and the Church. In practice we all tolerate, and many of us praise, Industrial Capitalism in its effects, while none of us can join its modern organized enemies, because its modern organized enemies proclaim a doctrine—to wit, the immorality of private property—which is in direct contradiction to Catholic morals.

Now look at the other side of the picture. Not only is Industrial Capitalism as a point of historical fact the product of that spirit which destroyed the Faith in men's hearts and eradicated it from society—where they could—by the most abominable persecutions; but, also in point of historical fact, Industrial

Capitalism has arisen late in societies of Catholic culture, has not flourished therein, and, what is more, in proportion as the nation is affected by Catholicism, in that proportion did it come tardily to accept the inroads of Industrial Capitalism and in that proportion does it still ill agree with Industrial Capitalism. That is why the more Catholic districts of Europe have in the past been called "backward"; and that is why there is a fiercer class war in the industrial plague spots of Catholic Europe than in the great towns of Protestant Europe.

In France, one of the main reasons why the anti-Catholic minority, especially the anti-Catholic of the Huguenot type, plays so great a part in the economic control of the country is that he has been the pioneer in introducing the mechanics of Industrial Capitalism. In Spain, Industrial Capitalism halts and occasions fierce revolts. It came very late to Italy; it has taken no strong root in Catholic Ireland; its triumphs have been everywhere the triumphs of the Protestant culture—in Prussianized Germany, in Great Britain, in the United States of America. The Calvinist has fitted in with it admirably and has indeed actively fostered it.

If we go behind the external phenomena and look at the workings of the mind we find the disagreement between Catholicism and Industrial Capitalism vivid and permanent. There is something irreconcilable between the one and the other. There is the point of Usury, which I have dealt with elsewhere, there is the all-important point of the Just Price, there is the point of the "*Panis Humanus*"—man's daily bread, the right possessed by the human being according to Catholic doctrine to live, and to live decently. There is the whole scheme of Catholic morals in the matter of justice, and particularly of justice in negotiation. There is even, if you will consider the matter with an active intelligence, underlying the whole affair the great doctrine of Free Will. For out of the doctrine of Free Will grows the practice of diversity, which is the deadly enemy of mechanical standardization, wherein Industrial Capitalism finds its best opportunity; and out of the doctrine of Free Will grows the revolt of the human spirit against restraint of will by that which has no moral authority to restrain it; and what moral authority has mere money? Why should I reverence or obey the man who happens to be richer than I am?

And, with that word "authority," one many bring in that other point, the Catholic doctrine of authority. For under Industrial Capitalism the command of men does not depend upon some overt political arrangement, as it did in the feudal times of Catholicism or in the older Imperial times of Catholicism, as it does now in the peasant conditions of Catholicism, but simply upon the ridiculous, bastard, and illegitimate power of mere wealth. For under Industrial Capitalism the power which controls men is the power of arbitrarily depriving them of their livelihood because you have control, through your wealth, of the means of livelihood and they have it not. Under Industrial Capitalism the proletarian tenant can be deprived of the roof over his head at the caprice or for the purely avaricious motives of a so-called master who is not morally a master at all; who is neither a prince, nor a lord, nor a father, nor anything but a credit in the books of his fellow capitalists, the banking monopolists. In no permanent organized Catholic state of society have you ever had citizens thus at the mercy of mere possessors.

Everything about Industrial Capitalism—its ineptitude, its vulgarity, its crying injustice, its dirt, its proclaimed indifference to morals (making the end of man an accumulation of wealth, and of labor itself an inhuman repetition without interest and without savor) is at war with the Catholic spirit.

What, then, are we to make of all this? Here is a conflict of spirits irreconcilable by their very nature. But we cannot engage in this conflict as it is now fought; we cannot take up the weapons ready to hand against Industrial Capitalism, because the weapons against Industrial Capitalism have been forged by men whose minds were of exactly the same heretical or anti-Catholic sort as those who framed Industrial Capitalism itself. What is called vaguely "Socialism," of which the only logical and complete form worthy of notice in practice is Communism, directly contradicts Catholic morals and is at definable and particular issue with them in a more immediate way than is capitalism.

Communism involves a direct and open denial of free will; and that it has immediate fruits violently in opposition to the fruits of Catholicism there can be no doubt. To put it more plainly, a Catholic supporting Communism is committing a mortal sin.

Further, to promote conflict between citizens, to engage in a class war with the destruction of capitalism *as the main end* is also directly in contradiction with Catholic morals. We may make war in defense of the Faith; we may make war against a direct denial of definable justice in a particular instance; but we may not say to the poor: "You have a right to fight the rich merely because they are rich and in order to make yourselves less poor." We may say: "You have a right to fight to prevent the conditions of your life becoming inhuman," but we may not say, "You have a right to fight merely because you desire to have more and your opponent to have less." It has been wittily and truly said that there has been only one Christian Socialist in history, and that even he did not try to be Christian and Socialist at the same time—the said individual being the penitent thief. He had the good fortune to be, while he was yet alive, promised Paradise by God Himself—but that was only after he had given up his Socialism. A very striking piece of recantation.[5]

Nevertheless, Catholics are forever in our time—or at least the more intelligent of them—seeking a way out. They are like men who find themselves in prison, who are forbidden by their very nature to break through the walls of that prison, but who grope for an exit of some kind, who are sure that somewhere they can find a door. Over and over again through the nineteenth and early twentieth centuries there have been Catholic efforts of this kind to escape from the injustice and degradations of Industrial Capitalism. Hitherto they have led to nothing.

---

5. Here I must repeat in another form what I said about Political labels in a former essay. I can conceive no sort of notion why an English Catholic should not vote, if he is fool enough to take that useless trouble, for a professional politician calling himself Socialist or Communist or Anarchist, as well as for one calling himself Unionist or Liberal. It can make no practical difference, and we all know very well that these terms as used in the puppet show at Westminster no longer represent realities.

One of the most remarkable was that propounded in some detail by Mr. Arthur Hungerford Pollen in a paper he read to the Wiseman society a few years ago. He put forth a detailed scheme which, as it is his and not mine, I will not here recapitulate, but of which the gist was the recognition of two things necessary to the reformation of our industrial society: (1) the sharing of the profits by the worker, and (2) the achievement of security by him; the stabilization of his economic position under such profit sharing. And the same authority has put forward privately in my hearing a very interesting form of this scheme under a particular name—"The Carpenter's Shop." All those who are making such attempts naturally rally round the *"Rerum Novarum"* of the great Pope Leo XIII, a document of great force to which our posterity will return and which was itself the product of the most eminent of Catholic minds and the chief authority of the Church approaching the problem.

In my judgment (and as this book is no more than a book of personal essays, I may be excused for putting forth a personal judgment), the essential of the effort must lie in our recognition of the true order of cause and effect. If we are to attack Industrial Capitalism we must do so because we are keeping in mind very clearly and continually the truth that religion is the formative element in any human society. Just as Industrial Capitalism came out of the Protestant ethic, so the remedy for it must come out of the Catholic ethic. *In other words, we must make the world Catholic before we can correct it from the evils into which the denial of Catholicism has thrown it.*

Consider what happened to the institution of slavery. The Church, when it began on earth its militant career, found slavery in possession. The antique world was a servile state; the civilized man of the Graeco-Roman civilization based his society upon slavery; so did (this must always be insisted upon because our textbooks always forget it) the barbarian world outside.

There were plenty of revolts against that state of affairs; there was to our knowledge one huge servile war, and there was protest of every kind by the philosophers and by individuals. But they had no success. Success in this field, though it came very slowly, was due to the conversion of the Roman Empire to Catholicism.

The Church did not denounce slavery, it accepted that institution. Slaves were told to obey their masters. It was one of their social duties, as it was the duty of the master to observe Christian charity towards his slave. It was part of good works (but of a rather heroic kind) to give freedom in bulk to one's slaves. But it was not an obligation. Slavery only disappeared after a process of centuries, and it only disappeared through the gradual working of the Catholic doctrine upon the European mind and through the incompatibility of that doctrine with such treatment of one's fellow men as was necessary if the discipline of servitude were to remain efficient. The slave of Pagan times was slowly transformed into the free peasant, but he was not declared free by any definite doctrine of the Church, nor at any one stage in the process would it have entered into the Catholic mind of the day to have said that slavery was in itself immoral. The freedom of the peasant developed as the beauty of external art developed in its Christian form, through the indirect working of the Catholic ethic.

In the absence, the gradual decline (where it is declining) of the Catholic ethic, slavery is coming back. Anyone with eyes to see can watch it coming back slowly but certainly—like a tide. Slowly but certainly the proletarian, by every political reform which secures his well-being under new rules of insurance, of State control in education, of State medicine and the rest, is developing into the slave, leaving the rich man apart and free. All industrial civilization is clearly moving towards the re-establishment of the Servile State, a matter I have discussed at greater length under the title of "the New Paganism."[6]

To produce the opposite of the Servile State out of the modern inhuman economic arrangement, the Church, acting as a solvent, is the necessary and the only force available. The conversion of society cannot be a rapid process, and therefore not a revolutionary one. It is therefore also, for the moment, an

6. Also in my book: *The Servile State.*

unsatisfactory process. But it is the right process. There is a very neat phrase which expresses the whole affair, "in better words than any poor words of mine," as the parson said in the story. These words are to be found in the vernacular translation of the New Testament. They are familiar to many of us. "Seek ye first the kingdom of God and its justice and all the rest shall be added unto you."

Begin by swinging society round into the Catholic course, and you will transmute Industrial Capitalism into something other, wherein free men can live, and a reasonable measure of joy will return to the unhappy race of men. But you must begin at the beginning.

A Letter To Dean Inge

The hatred of the Catholic Church, when it is expressed by a man of high culture, is at issue with that culture. It forbids him to say what he really thinks and it breeds in him a misapprehension of that from which this very culture proceeded.

15

A LETTER TO DEAN INGE

You have often attacked (and defamed) the Catholic Church in your pages. In that effort you have introduced, among others, my own less significant name. I propose to answer you.

The task is the easier because your animosity leads you to open declaration of your hatred, and, unlike too many of your kind, you are sometimes led by exasperation to be sincere.

Your indictment against the Faith (which you have also called "A bloody and treacherous corporation") is in these articles: that it is foreign, that it is disciplined, and that it is false—or (as you have written) "an imposture." The first is puerile, the second misconceived, the last momentous and the issue. I will take them in their order.

The Faith, you say, is foreign. Certainly it has been alienated by force and fraud from the English—but since how long? You know that it made England, and in particular remade England out of barbarism as no other province of our civilization was restored.

You are a man cultured and acquainted with the sources. You know well enough that England only *is* because the Church made England after the chaos of the fifth and sixth centuries. You know also—as your readers do not—that all about us, axe and ladder and saw, pillar and arch, and verse and law, and reasoning, are from that Mediterranean antiquity which the Church barely saved, and having saved, nourished into Christendom.

This done, England so recovered, the Faith presided over all her being for a thousand years. It was not till three hundred years ago that the half of England doubted. It is not two hundred since the last body of Englishmen loyal to the ancient national Faith of Englishmen were crushed out. A hideous official persecution, violent beyond example, and carried out in the interest of men newly enriched by the plunder of sacred things, took three lifetimes before it succeeded.

I find a contradiction in you here. An Englishman (you say) cannot be English unless he has in him some Manichean poison of the Puritans. So Chaucer, Alfred, Bede are not English? But next I hear that this Puritanism is a product of Englishry, so those thousand years *were* English after all—but, took their thousand years to bear the Protestant fruit, which blossomed suddenly three hundred years ago. When Shakespeare wrote, England was manifestly Catholic; when Milton, no longer. Yet you would abandon Shakespeare—with regret. You define an Englishman by his religion—no true Englishman can be of Shakespeare's mood, you say, only of Milton's. An Englishman of Shakespeare's mood, or Chaucer's, or More's, was no true Englishman.

The Englishman, groping for the light, shall no longer be English for you if he attains it. He shall only be English in your eyes on the condition of groping still. Certitude and the light upon eternal things are a bar to your granting a certificate of English essence.

What is more, the answer to the most universal (and most important) of questions must, you tell us, be local: and truth must be provincial to be true. If it oversteps national boundaries it is false. Was there ever such nonsense!

I have called it puerile—and so it is: a schoolboy's folly, to which all things not familiar seem ridiculous; for how can truth have local boundaries?

Your second objection is weightier. We of the Faith are not universal, but segregated. The world notes (as you do) that we stand together, making one regiment. You mistake that unity for mere servitude, and that bond for a chain. There is none of us but can assure you that only in the Faith does the reason reach a plenitude of freedom, nor any of us that has searched into ideas but will further tell you that we of the Faith may doubtfully admit some skeptics for our equals, but certainly no sentimentalists or men of merely emotional religion.

You say that we are within walls. So we are. But they are the walls of a city. It is the secure City of God. You resent our unity. Without it how would the structure of revelation be preserved, or of that Christian society which we made, which is Europe, and the dissolution of which would be the death of all? You are offended at our central command. But are we not under siege?

In truth it is not the constitution of the Church you abhor, but the thing itself—little though you know that thing: just as men hate some strange country though they know not a word of its language. When such decry the tyranny or the license of some polity, it is not Monarchy nor the Republic which troubles them, but the very texture of a detested nation. With you it is not the Captaincy of Peter that offends—though that is holy, necessary, and aboriginal—it is his Ship: the Ship itself: life on shipboard: the manner of the sea.

Wherein also resides your chief, and only grave, indeed your *one* grievance: that what the Catholic faith lays down, this you do not believe.

You have written "The Catholic Church is an Imposture," thereby provoking all the past of Europe, and challenging Ignatius of Antioch and Augustine of Hippo no less than the least of our fellowship today.

I forbear to pin you to a strict explanation, whether that "imposture" be the Incarnation, the Eucharist, or any other of our structural mysteries.

Your office forbids you to reply. You take money paid you to teach and maintain some, at least, of the Christian doctrines and the creeds. Therefore you cannot speak your mind openly, or tell us whether at heart you do not agree with the half-instructed millions around you who make no doubt that religion is of man: a figment.

I will content myself by concluding with this: that there wholly escapes you the character of the Catholic Church. You judge it by indications dead and valueless; you have not—for all your detestation of it—experienced its life, not known it for what it is. You are like one examining the windows of Chartres from within by candlelight, and marveling how any man can find glory in them; but we have the sun shining through. You are like one curious to note the canvas marks on the back of a Raeburn, and marveling to hear its obverse called the true picture of a man. For what is the Catholic Church? It is that which replies, coordinates, establishes. It is that within which is right order; outside, the puerilities and the despairs. It is the possession of perspective in the survey of the world. It is a grasp upon reality. Here alone is promise, and here alone a foundation.

Those of us who boast so stable an endowment make no claim thereby to personal peace; we are not saved thereby alone. But we are of so glorious a company that we receive support, and have communion. The Mother of God is also ours. Our dead are with us. Even in these our earthly miseries we always hear the distant something of an eternal music, and smell a native air. There is a standard set for us whereto our whole selves respond, which is that of an inherited and endless life, quite full, in our own country.

You may say, "All this is rhetoric." You would be wrong, for it is rather vision, recognition, and testimony. But take it for rhetoric. Have *you* any such? Be it but rhetoric, whence does that stream flow? Or what reserve is that which can fill even such a man as myself with fire? Can *your* opinion (or doubt, or gymnastics) do the same? I think not!

One thing in this world is different from all other. It has a personality and a force. It is recognized, and (when recognized) most violently loved or hated. It is the Catholic Church. Within that household the human spirit has roof and hearth. Outside it, is the Night.

In hac urbe lux sollennis,
Ver aeternum, pax perennis
*Et aeterna gaudia**.

---

*"Within this city are festive light, eternal truth, continual peace and everlasting joys." —*Editor*, 1992.

The Two Cultures Of The West

The true line of cleavage in Europe does not run between the various states, still less between various groups of languages, and not at all between various racial groups; Western Europe is essentially divided into two cultural groups, the difference between which has its origin in difference of religion. What stand opposed are the Catholic and the Protestant cultures; the latter—partly through the cooperation of England and Prussia, but more through the violent religious quarrel proceeding within the Catholic culture—long held the chief place. That Protestant hegemony in Europe is now ended.

16

THE TWO CULTURES OF THE WEST

Among the innumerable converging proofs which establish in a mind of sufficient experience the claims of the Catholic Church is its consonance with reality. It rings true to the world about us, and answers in harmony with it; so that, to the Catholic mind, things stand in their right proportion: the first, first, and the greater before the lesser. And this is true of all the main things of life, temporal as well as eternal.

It is a truth which applies even to political values; that is, to our estimate of human societies in their worldly relations.

Now, one of the tests of being in touch with reality is that such a position enables a man to think in the right categories. To think in false categories is the mark of error. Thus, if in attempting to distinguish between things of various kinds you get your lines of cleavage wrong, you are thinking in false categories; and in proportion as you mistake what the main lines of cleavage are—which are the greater, which the less—you fall into error upon the real distinction between one kind of thing and another, and you pay the penalty of error, which is false judgment with all its consequences.

For instance, supposing a foreigner be asked to write a report upon the different kinds of towns which he notices during travel through some country, and supposing he makes his categories alphabetical. He divides towns, in his report, according to the place in the alphabet of their first letters. He makes *that* the essential line of cleavage. He will clearly be wholly out of touch with reality. He will be completely in error. His conclusions will be worthless for political purposes, and those who commissioned him will, if they act upon such conclusions, make disastrous blunders in their policy.

He writes: "I distinguish between English towns in the first half of the alphabet, and towns in the second half. Birmingham, Chichester, Durham, are of one sort. They are first-class towns. Liverpool and Ludlow are marginal: neither of the first nor the second class. Portsmouth, Rochester, Repton, Sheffield are of the second class. Yarmouth and Alnwick are extreme cases of the difference between the two sorts of places. In the United States I put Concord and Bethlehem in the first class; Milwaukee is marginal; Reno and Philadelphia are of the second class, while Yuba and Atlanta are clearly extreme cases." Anyone acting upon such a report, let us say, for pushing the sales of new pills, would blunder enormously; he would spend a great deal of money at random.

Even if your foreign observer comes somewhat near reality, but is not in full touch with it, he will be still somewhat in error and his conclusions will mislead those who attempt to apply them.

Supposing, for instance, it is a question of selling electrical machinery, and he established his categories geographically, distinguishing between North England and South England. Such a distinction is much more real than an alphabetical distinction. The North of England is, in the main, of a sort different from the South; it is, in the main, the district of large industrial towns, while the South is more agricultural and what is called "residential."

He writes: "I advise pushing large dynamos in Alnwick, Buxton, and Huddersfield, but the smaller and cheaper are more suitable for Polperro, Brighton, Canterbury and London."

Those who commissioned him acting upon that advice would still be at sea; they might waste a great deal of energy in pushing huge dynamos upon the people of Penrith, and send little ones to Portsmouth.

To be in touch with reality in this case, the foreign observer would have to distinguish between large towns and small to begin with; to leave villages out of account. Only so could he give conclusions to be usefully acted upon.

Now, when we consider the present state of Christendom there is a certain main distinction of categories which is nearly always left out and the omission of which stultifies public judgment upon our international problem. This distinction is the distinction between the two types of religious culture into which Western Europe and its extensions overseas have fallen during the last three hundred years.

There is a Protestant culture and a Catholic culture. The difference between these two is the main difference dividing one sort of European from another. The boundary between the Catholic and Protestant cultures is *the* great line of cleavage, compared with which all others are secondary.

There are, of course, many other lines of cleavage established by languages and groups of languages. The British Isles are English speaking; they, with Holland, Scandinavia and Germany and the various German districts, have what are broadly called "Teutonic" forms of speech; while Spain, Italy and France have what are called "Latin" forms. That is a distinction with which everyone is familiar, and which is expressed in many popular maps.

Another line of cleavage very much more doubtful, and often fantastic, lies between what are thought to be racial differences. People are fond of distinguishing between "Celtic" and "Germanic" and "Slav" characteristics. Latterly there has arisen among silly pedantic people a talk of three supposed divisions, "Alpine," "Nordic" and "Mediterranean"; we shall not have long to wait for some new fashion in this sort of nonsense. It changes every few years.

A much more real distinction, but still a subsidiary one, is the distinction between various forms of Government. Some nations are called Monarchic, others Republican. Another distinction is between the theories of authority in government; some have a tradition of voting for sham representatives, others prefer a real executive in responsible hands. Another distinction much nearer reality is the distinction between industrial and agricultural communities.

But none of these categories have the same importance as the *religious*.

All social life is primarily conditioned by the mode of thought under which a society lives; its morals, its intellectual habits, its strong traditions of behavior, all these proceed from the religious doctrines under which it has been formed.

Those doctrines may have lost their original vitality. A nation once Calvinist in Creed may have ceased for the most part (as Scotland has) to believe in Predestination or to trouble about Conversion and the Reprobate sense; but it will continue for generations, and probably until a new set of doctrines shall be taught it, to think (therefore, to act) in the Calvinist manner. It will incline to the Calvinist attitude upon wealth and the acquirement thereof. It will take for granted an inexorable process of cause and effect. It will concentrate upon the responsibility of the individual to himself, the isolation of soul, and a consequent cultivation of what it will call "Character."

A nation like the French may largely lose the doctrine of the Incarnation and of the Immortality of the soul with its ultimate damnation or beatitude; but even those who have lost the whole Catholic scheme of doctrine still continue the Catholic habit. They will continue the Catholic sense that justice is more important than order; the Catholic tendency to well-divided property; and the Catholic conviction of Free will, with all the consequences that conviction entails in social habit. They may admit into their judicial code divorce and state education, but they will in practice condemn them to ridicule or repugnance and will maintain the sanctity of the family. In matters of money you will have, in the Catholic culture, the vice of avarice prominent; in the Protestant, rather, cupidity. In the Catholic culture men will envy wealth; in the Protestant they will pay it a sacramental respect. War will seem in the Protestant culture wrong in itself, because it is most painfully dangerous and will therefore only be waged against the weak. In the Catholic culture it will be admired or hated according to its object.

The whole tone and savor, the color of a community, on one side of this main line of cleavage is different from the tone, savor and color upon the other. There is far more fundamental difference between the mass of Irishmen and the mass of Englishmen, or between the mass of Poles and the mass of Pomeranian Germans, than between a Frenchman of the North and a Basque of Spain; though these two last live six hundred miles apart and are of alien blood and of utterly different speech.

All of this is true, of course, only of the bulk. It is not true of individuals. Further, there is in most districts some mixture of the two cultures. Nonetheless, the line of cleavage between the two, the Protestant and the Catholic cultures, is the main line of cleavage present in our civilization, and to neglect [this fact] is to misunderstand all international problems.

The Protestant culture in Europe is that of Great Britain, Holland and Scandinavia, the German Reich as organized by Bismarck, the Swiss Republic. The Catholic is that of France, and Belgium, Spain and Italy, Austria, Bohemia, Croatia, Styria, Poland.

But the Pattern is most complicated. England, with an intensely anti-Catholic tradition and spirit, has strong historical memories of Catholicism. Holland, though anti-Catholic by historical tradition, is numerically Catholic as to two-fifths of its people. Bismarck's "Reich"—upon which major section of the German race his genius imposed the general name of "Germany"—was carefully designed to include as large a proportion of Catholics as possible (one-third), subject to their remaining subordinate to Protestant Prussia. In the Swiss confederation, though the Protestants give the tone, the Catholic cantons have large autonomous powers. In France the Huguenots, perhaps a twentieth of the population, have a large portion of the financial power in their hands, strongly influence the university and color all legislation.

In the Protestant culture there is unity of aim; for, in the main, the temporal ideals released by the Reformation are at one, and the commercial spirit, the conception of what character should be, the things sought in social structure and ideal are in common. In the Catholic culture it is otherwise. The very unity and discipline of the Catholic Church, its divine claims (which sound to all not of its allegiance intolerably arrogant) cause to rise against it an intense opposition. In most societies of Catholic culture today power is in the hands of men who, while for the most part of Catholic tradition in morals and social philosophy, are what is called "Anti-Clerical," that is, determinedly and often fanatically determined upon the destruction of the Faith in men's minds. This presence of anti-Catholic governments in Catholic countries forms the chief paradox of our times, or, at least, of the times immediately past; for the Great War [World War I], coming at the end of, and accentuating a certain change in all this has had a profound effect in modifying the old war between "Liberalism" and the Church: so that today the new war on the Church in Spain looks belated and out of date. To this "attack from within" the Protestants who were nationals of Catholic countries naturally allied themselves, as did—as naturally—the Jews. But also, oddly enough, the Masonic organization, though having nothing in its constitution specifically opposed to the Church, became everywhere, not only identified with anti-clericalism, but the ferment and the directing force of it.

In such a state of affairs—the Catholic culture, since the early eighteenth century divided against itself, and most so in the nineteenth century, the Protestant culture mainly homogeneous—hegemony fell to the latter. In Europe, London and Berlin as cities, the English gentry and the Prussian monarchy as social forces, were the two poles of anti-Catholic effort. Economically the Protestant culture came to outweigh by far the Catholic and in the world of ideas it dominated. Its institutions spread to, its ideas mixed awkwardly with, the materially declining Catholic world. In arms the effect was enhanced by the success of Protestant Prussia. The Catholic Rhineland had been given to Prussia after the defeat of Napoleon. Prussia destroyed the power of Catholic Austria in 1866, and four years later the complete victory over France founded Bismarck's "Reich," with its subjection of the Catholic upper Danube and the rest to the Protestant Hohenzollern influence. New, united Italy had arisen in spite of the Church. France, after defeat, fell into moral disunion.

Spain decayed. Catholic Poland and Ireland were enslaved. The tide ran at full strength against the traditional Catholic culture of Europe. But it came to high water; and tides turn. It was already apparent, in the first decade of the new century, that the Catholic culture, badly outrun by the industrialized Britain and North Germany of the nineteenth century, but much more weakened by its permanent internal quarrel, was changing. It had itself been increasingly industrialized, and, for the first time in some two hundred years, a rift was developing between England and Prussia. Meanwhile, the climax of anti-clericalism in the Catholic culture which was reached after the Dreyfus case and which all but destroyed religious education in France, provoked a reaction which has steadily increased from that day to this. What the fortunes of that French Catholic reaction may be we know not, but it is still going forward. The intellectual life of France, in which the Faith had lost ground for nearly two centuries, began to consider a partial return. It was not thorough, still less was it homogeneous; the mass of what was official in the instructed classes remained opposed to the Church, and the University, though divided, was preponderantly anti-Catholic; but the tone of writing and conversation moved to the right. Then arose a fashion of sympathy for Catholicism among the doubters; there was an increasing connection between national feeling and the Church. The influence of Louvain, the resurrection of Scholasticism, Cardinal Mercier, had much to do with this, but more that mysterious influence of changing mood the origins of which can never be found in external things. The hearty contempt felt for Parliament, and the close connection between Parliamentary Masonic caucuses and anti-Clericalism, helped the movement.

It was not powerful, still less universal; it was largely dilettante, and it was badly inmixed with motives in no way Catholic—but it was appreciable. Unfortunately, it did not affect the masses, whom the Masonic control of popular education steadily alienated from religion.

Then came the War [World War I]. The War accentuated all pre-War tendencies—in social structure as in Philosophy. It accentuated this movement in France and Belgium. In Italy it led, as we know, to the destruction of the Masonic regime. It liberated Poland and, in part, Ireland; by producing Soviet Communist rule in Russia it warned the Agnostic Capitalism of the West, and led them to fear, indirectly, the consequences of its old antagonism to religion. It was clearly apparent after the War that the Church was the bulwark of Society and that to continue at odds with it was to invite revolution. The old hatred of the Church still worked in the Peace Treaties. The nations of Protestant culture succeeded in saving the Reich; French anti-clericals with Clemenceau at their head most suicidally prevented the union of Bavaria with Austria, ruined the Hapsburg throne, supported the Masonic clique in Bohemia and unnaturally attached the Southern Catholic Slavs to the alien culture of Belgrade. But the main outstanding fact of the War which overshadows all other issues was the defeat of Prussia—the very core of the Protestant culture. Bismarck's artificial Reich survived, and, on paper, Berlin was stronger in the Constitution than ever; but the moral and intellectual prestige of Berlin had passed. There is no sign of their returning.

To sum up: the hegemony of the Protestant culture in Europe has crumbled. A strong new Italy, a less divided France, a free Poland and a mainly free Ireland are the symbols, politically, of what has happened. The strength of the Protestant culture now lies out of Europe, in the United States.

But this great change does not mean that the Catholic Church is to be stronger politically in Europe. There remains, potential where the battle has lulled, actual where it has flamed up again (as, at the moment of writing, in Spain), the anti-clerical power with its Masonic organization and nucleus everywhere standing throughout the Catholic culture side by side with, and mortally opposed to, the Catholic Church. No one can tell when the struggle may not be renewed or what its issue will be.

What we can say of the future—and the only thing we can say—is that, of the two cultures, the long supremacy of the Protestant one in Europe is over; its reliance must henceforward be on American influence, while the Catholic one is still undecided between a reaction towards its great origins in religion and a popular drift still farther away from these—which drift, if it becomes the main stream, will carry our civilization into the abyss. For upon the maintenance and increase of the Church, the life of our civilization depends. There are apparent in all art, literature and morals many forerunners of collapse. Whether we shall avoid it or succumb, none can tell.

ABOUT THE AUTHOR

Hilaire Belloc
1870-1953

The great Hilaire Belloc was likely the most famous and influential Catholic historian of the past two centuries. His rare understanding of the central role of the Catholic Faith in forming Western Civilization—from the time of Christ up to our own—still opens the eyes of many today.

Hilaire Belloc was born in 1870 at La Celle, St. Cloud, France. His father was a distinguished French lawyer; his mother was English. After his father's death, the family moved to England. Hilaire did his military service in France, then returned to Balliol College, Oxford, taking first-class honors in history when he graduated in 1895. It has been said that his ambition was to rewrite the Catholic history of his two fatherlands, France and England. In 1896 he married Elodie Hogan of Napa, California; the marriage was blessed with two sons and two daughters.

During a period of 50 years—until he suffered a stroke in 1946—Hilaire Belloc wrote over a hundred books on history, economics, military science and travel, plus novels and poetry. He also wrote hundreds of magazine and newspaper articles. He served for a time as a member of the English House of Commons and edited a paper called the *Eye-Witness.*

As an historian, Belloc is largely responsible for correcting the once nearly universal *Whig* interpretation of British history, which attributed Britain's greatness to her Anglo-Saxon and Protestant background.

Hilaire Belloc visited the United States several times, giving guest lectures at both Notre Dame and Fordham Universities. Among his most famous books are *The Great Heresies, Survivals and New Arrivals* (something of a sequel to the above), *The Path to Rome, Characters of the Reformation,* and *How the Reformation Happened.* Hilaire Belloc died in 1953, leaving behind a great legacy of insight regarding the true, though largely unrecognized, inspirer of Western Civilization—the Catholic Church.